Polemics

Political Poems & Prose

2016–2025

Andrea W LeDew

Polemics: Political Poems & Prose

2016-2025

Andrea W LeDew

Andrea W LeDew

Copyright © 2025 by Andrea W LeDew.

All rights reserved.

No portion of this book may be reproduced in any form without written permission from the publisher or author, except as permitted by U.S. copyright law.

Any use of this publication to "train" artificial intelligence (AI) technologies to generate text is expressly prohibited. The author reserves all rights to license uses of this work for generative AI training and development of machine learning models.

Dedicated
to my dear husband, *who,*
despite his inborn preference for a clear, concise memo,
has endured my wordy ramblings,
replete with subordinate clauses, semicolons,
intricate metaphors, meandering descriptions,
and even the occasional pronoun, lacking
—God forbid!—
a clear antecedent.

***

Be it acknowledged, that
for supporting me throughout life, in every possible way,
and most especially,
for adding four precious souls to my world
—broadening my perspective, as well as my waistline—
I am forever in his debt.

***

Also,
a special thank you
to those of you who vote.
We need you.

Contents

Caveat	1
1. Election Eve 2016 Intro	5
Election Eve 2016	6
2. Doing Nothing Intro	8
Doing Nothing	9
3. The Line Intro	10
The Line	11
4. Playing in a Minefield Intro	13
Playing in a Minefield	14
5. Death and Other Ailments Intro	17
Death and Other Ailments	19
6. River of Grass Intro	26
River of Grass	28

7. The Wardrobe of Kings Intro	33
The Wardrobe of Kings	35
8. Statues Intro	38
Statues	40
9. The Yoke Intro	42
The Yoke	43
10. Scrooge Intro	45
Scrooge	46
11. On Pharaoh's Watch Intro	48
On Pharaoh's Watch	50
12. Dominate Intro	52
Dominate	54
13. Suddenly Silent Intro	57
Suddenly Silent	58
14. Smoky Intro	60
Smoky	61
15. Debatable Intro	62
Debatable	64
16. All Made Up Intro	66
All Made Up	67
17. Electoral Intro	68
Electoral	70

18. Great Patriots Intro	72
Great Patriots	75
19. Interregnum Intro	77
Interregnum	78
20. Q & A Intro	80
Q & A	82
21. Waste Intro	84
Waste	85
22. The Mighty Intro	87
The Mighty	88
23. Round Two Intro	90
Round Two	92
24. Minor Edits Intro	95
Minor Edits	97
25. A Vote Intro	99
A Vote	101
26. Liberal Wish List Intro	103
Liberal Wish List	104
27. Public Servant Intro	106
Public Servant	108
28. Public Square Intro	110
Public Square	112

29. The Racket Intro	114
The Racket	115
30. Burning Flags Intro	117
Burning Flags	119
31. Foul Ball Intro	122
Foul Ball	123
32. Frat Boy Intro	126
Frat Boy	128
33. Flies Intro	130
Flies	132
34. Returning Boots Intro	134
Returning Boots	136
35. Regrets Intro	138
Regrets	139
36. The Lawman Intro	142
The Lawman	143
37. Déjà vu Intro	146
Déjà vu	148
38. False Equivalencies Intro	150
False Equivalencies	152
39. Grateful Intro	154
Grateful	155

40. Litmus Test Intro	158
Litmus Test	160
41. Scores Intro	162
Scores	164
42. Dystopia Today Intro	167
Dystopia Today	170
43. Remarkably Indecent Intro	172
Remarkably Indecent	174
44. Free Speech Intro	176
Free Speech	178
45. The Swindler Intro	180
The Swindler	182
46. Who Owns My Vote? Intro	185
Who Owns My Vote?	187
47. The End Intro	192
The End	193
48. Ampersands Intro	195
Ampersands	197
49. Kangaroo Court (Honeypot) Intro	199
Kangaroo Court (Honeypot)	200
50. Gray Galleons Intro	202
Gray Galleons	203

51. First At Last Intro	206
First At Last	207
52. Laughing Intro	209
Laughing	210
53. White Intro	212
White	213
54. Bitch Intro	215
Bitch	216
55. Weird Intro	220
Weird	221
56. One More Intro	226
One More	227
57. No More Intro	234
No More	235
58. News from the Front: JaxbyJax 2024 Intro	237
News from the Front: JaxbyJax 2024	238
59. Just Wait and See Intro	241
Just Wait and See	242
60. A Cold New Year's in Florida Intro	244
A Cold New Year's in Florida	245
61. Half-Mast Intro	247
Half-Mast	248

62. Private School Intro	250
Private School	251
63. Left Unattended Intro	253
Left Unattended	254
64. It Should Be Free Intro	256
It Should Be Free	257
65. Country, In the Strictest Sense of the Word Intro	259
Country, In the Strictest Sense of the Word	261
66. Fire Ants Intro	272
Fire Ants	273
67. Butterfly Whispers Intro	275
Butterfly Whispers	276
68. Five Things Intro	279
Five Things	280
69. Porch Protest Intro	283
Porch Protest	284
70. Playing Cards Intro	298
Playing Cards	299
71. Radio Free Europe Intro	301
Radio Free Europe	302
72. Lunatic Intro	304
Lunatic	306

73. Insecure Intro	308
Insecure	309
74. In a Red District (Represent) Intro	311
In a Red District (Represent)	312
75. Liberation Day (April 2, 2025) Intro	315
Liberation Day (April 2, 2025)	316
76. Doors and Windows Intro	318
Doors and Windows	319
77. Scream Intro	321
Scream	323
78. Pining Intro	328
Pining	329
The Author: Andrea W LeDew	333
What You Will Find Inside	336

Caveat

Polemics: Political Poems & Prose by Andrea W. LeDew is a dated political journal with a liberal bent. The word ***polemic*** means controversial argument.

This collection explores controversial issues and events in the order in which they appeared on the American scene. It portrays the period between November 2016 and April 2025 in the United States. Taking the reported facts of news stories as her starting point, the author interprets and expands upon them, as her logic and fancy dictate.

Most of the seventy-eight works are rhyming poems, but the collection also contains several essays and a single short story. The works were all contemporaneously written, in response to events.

For each piece, there is a short intro. It outlines basic events upon which the piece is based. In older works, the inciting incidents may have faded from memory, so a lightly-edited version of the original intro from the author's website *For Random Learning Comes,* is included. Most of the pieces in this collection previously appeared there. More recent works receive only a short blurb, by way of introduction.

These pieces have been chosen for their political nature. The collection does not include all work by the author during this period.

The pieces were not written to pick a fight, but instead, to record the author's immediate reactions to events. Such writing is based on subjective impressions and perceptions, and inevitably will betray the bias of a particular point of view. Some of these points of view have unfortunately not weathered the test of time very well.

It is questionable, whether objective truth *can* be observed or experienced. It is also sometimes unclear to what extent the media reports facts faithfully and accurately. Nonetheless, poetry and prose inspired by reported events may unintentionally reveal some deeper truth.

When, as in our age, truth is often taken for lies, and lies for truth, nothing feels truer to us than our own feelings, beliefs and opinions. The author has sought to record hers as best she could, given the strictures of talent, rhyme and the English language. In the end, all opinions expressed here are *hers*.

Public figures are often alluded to in this collection. Please note that they are depicted, more or less, as *caricatures*. Any unreported, behind-the-scenes moments or attributed thoughts are *presumed* and *based only on conjecture and fantasy*.

None of this poetry or prose is meant to be interpreted as fact. It is an attempt at art. Or, at the very most prosaic, an attempt at commentary. Likewise, no legal advice or legal opinion is contained in the text. It is neither offered nor intended as such, and should *not* be relied upon in any way.

You may disagree with the sentiments in this collection, or you may be persuaded by them. Either way, as a proud American or as a fan of American values, you should be willing to defend to the death, the right we each have, to express them.

These pieces have acted as the author's companions during a profoundly mystifying political period. They have assisted her in making some sense of events. Writing this collection and sharing it with you has also given her a welcome chance to protest and reject the manifold dubious practices which seem to be harming her country.

POLEMICS: POLITICAL POEMS & PROSE

May this collection also provide comfort and courage to you, on your own journey.

Andrea W LeDew

Election Eve 2016 Intro

11/7/2016

It is now sixty days before our presidential election (September 2020) and I thought I might take a trip down memory lane in the next few weeks, with poems, stories and blogposts I have written during the Trump Presidency. Most of them were influenced by current events at the time and so will serve as a reminder of what these years have been like.

This one is set on the night before Election Day, 2016 and was written at about that time. I recall hearing a commentator use the phrase, "I weep for the nation and the world," and the poem grew from there.

Election Eve 2016

I weep for the nation and the world.
For what will come Election Night?
A white-hot flame. Dumb lava, bright,
Will burn away our every right,
Will blow up government, and despite
All pride, consume our Flag, unfurled.

I weep for the nation and the world.
The choice is clear for all to see:
A queen versus mediocrity;
Bombast versus ways and means;
Experience versus hateful speech.
They say it's close. Our fingers curl.

I weep for the nation and the world.
But who's to blame for this sad state?
Who clutched at comments, full of hate?
Who broadcast rallies—and "debates"
That failed the promise of the name?
Reporters sat and knit and purled.

I weep for the nation and the world.
How must our Allies gauge this breeze,
As slyly smile our enemies?
So do the Mighty fall, and trees
Once grand and great, rot with disease.
Welcome him, our nation's Leading Churl.

Doing Nothing Intro

12/31/2016

    This poem is set on New Year's Eve 2016, before our President took office in January. It was written at about the same time.

Doing Nothing

We have no plans for New Year's Eve:
No gaudy, grand, peculiar Eve;
No sparkly, wild, and drunken night;
No revels till the early light.

We have no plans for New Year's Eve:
We watch, alone, the Year's reprieve,
While headlights stream on past at dusk,
As fireworks burst, in a sudden thrust.

But what have we to say to Thee,
New Year, as we peer in disbelief?
Good Riddance?

For Pity's sake, drop that ball!
In doing nothing, we did it all.

The Line Intro

2017

    This tongue-in-cheek poem deals with the recurring themes of immigration and racial tensions, and whether we consider ourselves gracious hosts who welcome outsiders, or whether we are even willing to accept and include those who live in our midst, but look or act different.

    "Differentiation" is a term commonly used in the world of special education, to describe the practice of adapting educational content to suit the unique strengths and needs of each learner. In common parlance, the word means to distinguish and separate things into different groups. This is the definition the speaker (who does not represent my point of view!) seems to reference.

The Line

We need to differentiate
Between the curvy and the straight,
Between the zigzag and the line
That falters not a step behind,
And never varies its inflection,
Infinite, in both directions.

We need to make the difference clear
Between that other place, and here.
With all those shipping to our shores—
The nation foreigners adore—
We need to keep their papers straight:
We need to differentiate.

We cannot let them blur the line,
The black and white, the yours and mine.

We cannot let them in, not one,
Full-knowing gain is zero-sum.
Soon no one will be left in sight
Except the ones who left the Right.

Though you may call it racist hate:
I beg to differentiate.

Playing in a Minefield Intro

5/29/2017

    This post was originally published around Memorial Day 2017 as a response to the prompt "Detonate." It touches upon our relationship to the outside world, our sense of ourselves as heroes, and our terror in the face of those who might seek to harm us. Now (in 2020) our heroes also include all those who help defend us from the coronavirus.

    International relations seem to be deteriorating, no matter how Great we think we've made America. But thank you anyway, to all the heroes, even though this may be the wrong three-day weekend for it!

Playing in a Minefield

Heroes

Today, Memorial Day, we remember the ones who perished. The ones who put themselves in peril for our sake. The ones who paid for our liberty with their lives.

My husband's grandfather was one such man. He flew at the Battle of Midway and perished in the fight. My mother-in-law grew up without a father from the age of 12. She christened a ship in his name and later a bridge. We have a shrine, of sorts, in our house. He deserves to be remembered.

When men and women die, protecting us and our country, we celebrate them as heroes. Would we ourselves be able to summon such courage, or be so willing to sacrifice?

When someone dies senselessly in an attack by terrorists, we consider them heroes too. We build monuments and we mourn, for all they could still have done, had their lives not been cut short. And those who perish in the course of responding to the attack are our heroes too.

Hard to imagine taking on a mission where return is uncertain. Would we be willing to fly the plane if there was not enough gas to get back? Would we march into the flames?

There was a Need

On *The Greatest Generation*, Tom Brokaw's documentary, one veteran put it more or less this way: We did it because there was a need. They needed pilots, so up we went, training or no training.

Their bravery astounds those of us who have never experienced war. Not close up, anyway. But for the ones who did the job, it was probably more like putting one foot in front of the other. It needed to be done. And so, they did it.

Romanticizing War

Yet it is one-sided to romanticize war. While we celebrate the victories, we must remember. Where there are winners, there are always losers.

Last night I was watching CNN's *Parts Unknown* with Anthony Bourdain. Laos looks like a lovely place, and of course the food looks great.

But it was eerie to watch the interviews with survivors of the conflict we know as the Vietnam War. The contemporaries of Baby Boomers, bearing the scars of war.

The US bombed them. But then the US helped them afterwards. They seemed, at least on camera, to bear no grudges. Hard to imagine Americans being so forgiving.

Most horrible of all was the realization that, because of that war, because of us, there are still millions of undetonated shells littering the countryside, despite crews trying to remove them every day.

Hidden booby traps. Waiting.

And even to this day, children are the most frequent victims. Their own desire to play puts them in peril.

Perish the Thought

My first awareness of terrorism was little more than a childhood sense that the Middle East was always in conflict, would forever be in conflict. Then as I grew older, a vague idea of hijackers and Patty Hearst.

The first real immediate threat I ever felt was when I was in Germany, and we were expecting a visitor to arrive by plane. Then we heard the news over the radio that a bomb had been found at the airport. Hours passed before we knew whether our visitor was safe.

Those were strange days to be an American in Germany, much like today, I imagine. An unpopular president held the reigns of our country then: unpopular abroad, that is. I'm sure Trump would not mind the comparison to Reagan.

But, at the time, most of my German friends thought that a nuclear World War Three was about to be fought between the Soviet Union and the US. Right there on German soil.

Since I've had children, the threats in the US and Europe seem to have increased in frequency. Oklahoma City, 9/11 and only in the past few years, many European targets have been hit, with fatal effects. Places I used to think of as safe. Places I would like to show my children someday.

Unlike the attacks of states, who have threatened America in the past, these attacks seem more indirect. Who the victim is, is not important. Only, that there be victims.

They seek to make us afraid. They want us to watch our step. They want us to question whether it's safe out there.

Their grievances and their anger still survive, years and years after whatever conflict first inspired them to hate us. They hold a grudge.

And they randomly pepper the landscape of our civilized world with buried landmines, ready to explode, at the slightest trigger.

Hidden booby traps. Waiting.

And we just want to play.

Death and Other Ailments Intro

8/14/2017

I first published this essay in August of 2017, in response to the Charlottesville debacle. At the risk of having this be perceived as little different than our President's own comment, that "There are good people on both sides," I tried at that time to convey my conflicted emotions on the subject of Confederate Statuary.

As a white Yankee transplant who has lived most of her life in the South, with no known Confederate ancestry, I'm still a bit squeamish about iconoclasm of any kind. I tend to err on the side of preservation, both of art and history, no matter how flawed the underlying premise, or intended symbolism, may happen to be.

Naturally, more recent events have turned the tide on this once controversial issue, and that has led to the removal of many of the very monuments that caused such a fuss in the first place. This makes my point, if I had one, somewhat moot.

Death and Other Ailments

When I was in law school, I had the good fortune to be chosen as a research assistant to a law professor who was trying to write a book on Plain English. This was the late 80's.

I was a fair to middling law student, and was quite thrilled to have been chosen for anything. The competition in that "Type-A" commune was that fierce. Others grasped for the brass ring, battling for positions on law review, or vying for clerkships. It was all I could do, to avoid dying of boredom, sifting through cases and statutes as dry as dust, desperately seeking to uncover the gems of wisdom, hidden therein.

Plain English

The *Plain English Movement* probably had the side effect of making the lives of subsequent law students a bit easier. But primarily, it benefited the common man. The idea was to take archaic legalese and turn it into something generally comprehensible. A very laudable ambition, although I cannot say that it has been completely realized.

My job had less to do with content, and more to do with indexing the compendium, but I felt proud to be part of such an effort. Prior to the Plain English Movement, and the simplification of documents, it was probably much harder for a layperson to litigate a case *pro se* (not that it's wise to do so now). *Legal Zoom* and similar do-it-yourself sites might well never have happened, without it.

Today, at least, you can read through the Plain English summary of many documents and understand the basic terms of your loans (or mortgages, or credit cards or leases). Before you sign on the dotted line.

Things have definitely improved. Though many, if not most people, still don't read before they sign or click "Agree."

No Remedy for Legal Writing

Legal language has a way of gumming up the gears of comprehension. I'm not sure if it is a factor of the words themselves, or of the way they are, sometimes inexpertly, strung together.

As an English major, I had particular trouble with this in law school. In fact, when I was admitted, I was told I would have to take a remedial writing class. Apparently my LSAT essay score showed that I would be less than successful at legal writing.

This was an insult of the highest order. I dug my heels in. I ignored the recommendation.

Perhaps to my own detriment. Legal writing was harder than I thought. There is a certain level of discipline required, an impatience for extraneous facts, emotions, opinions or attitudes. And at least at the law school level, there is a dislike for flowery language of any kind.

That is, of course, the exact type of language that English majors are trained, and encouraged, and certified, to use.

Just the Facts Ma'am.

Law School was a bully. It was as if my old Argumentative and Persuasive Writing class during undergrad had been working out at the gym. It had gained muscle. And now, it was pushing me around.

Legal writing is not usually a meandering, friendly sort of thing. It is purposeful. And usually one-sided. It is a weapon designed to fatally wound its target. It is a barbed wire fence, built around the client, for the sole purpose of protecting him, at the expense of all others. It is a supplication, designed to manipulate the heartstrings of those who read or hear it, in order to draw them over to a point of view more sympathetic to the client.

It has its place.

The Impediment of Writing "Well"

I experienced a lot of growing pains, trying to adjust to the demands of this new genre. Spending four years reading novels and poetry was no preparation for interpreting these harsh, discordant voices, obscurely wrestling arcane concepts into modern molds.

And yet the writing could be beautiful at times. Some of the judges and justices were eloquent and precise and flawlessly logical, even when introducing brand new principles. Metaphor was carried, in some decisions, to new heights.

My Legal Writing class was not the only one in which my English major became an impediment.

My Property professor, God rest his soul, singled us out by major on the first day of class. Engineers, business majors, computer science geeks—these would do well in his class, he predicted. Those of us with liberal arts degrees were destined to flounder.

And flounder I did. That class is responsible for most of my "missed exam" nightmares, to this day. I did not truly understand the concept of the entail, until I watched Downton Abbey.

Seriously Ridiculous

Because of this background of being tortured, slowly, into producing a (barely) respectable version of legal writing, I am very alert to silly formulations and unintended meanings in documents penned by a lawyer's hand.

The latest one I found was in a waiver of liability. You cannot throw a cat without hitting some place that will demand such a waiver from you. A gym, a school, a church for homeschool coop, an outdoor event for children. Swimming was actually forbidden on field trips by our school district because of one accident, long ago, in which a child died. I am absolutely all for the safety of children, of adults even, although I think we are often being protected only from ourselves. But surely danger cannot be entirely legislated or drafted out of existence? And fault shouldn't be.

Anyway, this waiver contained the following language:

> "...my participation...and/or use of such equipment may result in [long list of horrible injuries], **death or other ailments that could cause serious disability**..."

The lack of an Oxford comma in this series makes all the difference.

If they had put a comma in after the word "death," it would not have caught my eye.

But just the phrase: "death or other ailments!" It is laughable to include death among sicknesses and injuries infinitely less final, as if death were an illness to be recovered from, given enough time and the proper care.

But then, to say that "death...could cause serious disability" is even more ridiculous. Such a disability would be serious indeed.

The Disability of Death

This made me contemplate the disability caused by Death.

Indulge me here. Obviously, Death is an impediment to doing many things. Speaking, for instance. Expressing your opinion. Arguing your case. Objecting to things going on around you.

Charlottesville, Virginia has had a very tough weekend, with horrible unforeseen events swirling around the attempt to make history "right" somehow.

Is it right when we remember history, and commemorate it, by preserving monuments put up by earlier generations, regardless of what they stand for? Should we preserve history, warts and all?

Or is it right when we undo the overzealousness of a less inclusive, agenda-packed, earlier era (such as Jim Crow) and tear down its monuments (to the Civil War) because we now believe they were erected for the wrong reasons (to humiliate, subjugate and keep a class of people "in their place?")

It makes me wonder what the dead would say.

- The poor woman who gave her life so needlessly. I would not presume to guess at her words.

- Thomas Jefferson, the slave owner and statesman, founder of the University of Virginia. An outstanding and accomplished man. But, in his complicated relationship with race, no more honorable than other white men of his time and class. What would he say, had he witnessed this "peaceful" protest and counter-protest, this "expression" of free speech and the right to assemble, turned violent?

- Robert E. Lee, the brilliant general who fought for the losing side. The side we now revile, looking on it with our 21st century eyes. Because of its efforts to preserve slavery, a shameful economic institution, blighted by corruption and human rights abuse. What would he say, of this effort to obliterate the memory of his military service?

And what about the many, many other, more humble-born, dead?

- The Confederate soldier ancestors of people across the country. Some of their progeny cherish the mementos or memories of their brave lost forefathers and mothers. They consider them none the less brave, even though they fought for a cause and a way of life that, in part, espoused both cruelty and bigotry.

- The slave ancestors of people across the country. Their progeny live, today, in a country still filled with discrimination based on race. The continued exaltation in statuary of those same villains, who fought to continue their ancestors' complete oppression, in a war that bought them only slightly more freedom, and far less than full equality, probably feels like insult following injury.

Righting and Writing History

Through modern media, straight from Charlottesville, VA, the most extreme views are on display every hour. White Supremacists who want the South to rise again. People who want to erase the Confederacy from the record book, as if this would somehow undo all that has gone before. And a few moderate voices, suggesting change, suggesting amendment, suggesting education.

I live in a Southern town with questionable statues. I am a transplant, a Yankee who imitated Southern voices as a child, thinking a Southern accent made people sound stupid. I remember thinking, how could they allow that to happen, those stupid Southerners. Surely they knew, like we did Up North, that slavery was bad? How could they perpetuate it, profit from it? How could they fight a war defending it? As if we Yankees were somehow free from sin!

I hear these kinds of comments from my kids all the time. When you are removed by a generation or more, you cannot fathom what could lead them to such idiocy. This is the province of historians, and only they can pretend to grapple with such questions.

- Why didn't women always work?

- Why did the Holocaust happen?

- Why did we go to Vietnam?

Impossible questions to answer. You had to be there.

To me, the message to be learned from all this is this:

Regardless of what the living want, the dead would want their story to be told.

All of it. All of them.

But they can't say. They don't have a voice. Because of Death and other ailments.

River of Grass Intro

2/15/18

    This essay was first published in early 2018, the day after the Parkland massacre in South Florida. A young man returned to his high school--named after Marjory Stoneman Douglas. She was the author of ***The Everglades: River of Grass,*** a scientific love song to the Florida Everglades. The young man then proceeded to open fire, killing seventeen students.
    With all the chants of "Drain the Swamp," and the cozy relationship of the current president with the National Rifle Association, I have chosen to include a reminder of this ever-present threat of violence, and its costs.
    Whether you call it gun control or protecting our Second Amendment freedoms, this debate has served to divide us into opposing camps, each furiously doing nothing about it.

Meanwhile, we watch the number of victims inexorably rise, much like the deficit clock. Ironic, that the school's namesake is heralded as a founding member of the environmental movement. Which our president seems equally to despise.

This is a reminder that we want our leadership to preserve and nurture all our natural resources, whether they be water, plant, animal, or human.

River of Grass

I first read Margory Stoneman Douglas's book, *The Everglades: River of Grass (1947)* in my late twenties, while working in South Florida. My husband and I, and, eventually, our first-born girl, lived outside Fort Lauderdale in one of the western suburbs. Hugging the Everglades itself, on its western flank, Coral Springs was just a few miles north, and near to it, an area called Parkland.

As I recall, the book was slim and very readable, and extremely motivating for a brand-new lawyer like me, interested in environmental issues. At the time, there was the threat of offshore oil drilling, and I remember going to a rally to protest such an abomination. Of course, this was long before Deep Water Horizon turned our worst fears into reality.

That was my only environmental protest, unless you count the time I tagged along, in the mid-eighties, to protest nuclear weapons stored on a US military base in Heilbronn, Germany. That could only have been called "environmental" to the extent that the potential was there, with missiles pointing from both the West and the East, to destroy the entire environment known as Europe.

The Cold War was a scary time, to be sure, although the permafrost was already thawing by the time I had any awareness of the threat. A popular song of the era was Sting's song about impending nuclear war, *Russians*. Its chorus emphasized how the universal impulse to care for our kids is our best protection from nuclear annihilation.

Turning a Frog into a Prince

Wikipedia's entry on Marjory Stoneman Douglas says her book "redefined the popular conception of the Everglades as a treasured river instead of a worthless swamp." Unlike many states, which have mostly dry land, a large amount of Florida prior to the twentieth century was swampy wetlands. The "river" she talked about started in Lake Okeechobee and flowed south, ever widening, to engulf most of South Florida in a soggy, grassy soup.

Many who have lived in Florida have made the trek across Alligator Alley, the road connecting the Southeast Florida cities of Miami, Fort Lauderdale and Palm Beach, with the West Coast cities of Naples, Fort Meyers and further north, Tampa/St. Pete. In the eighties, you drove for miles and miles, and there was nothing around you but a flat wasteland of waving swamp grass.

The attitude toward the environment, early on in the twentieth century, was much like our current President's attitude, regarding the federal government. Calls to "Drain the Swamp!" caused Florida endless environmental indignities. Suburbs and even cities were built on wet ground with tons of fill dirt. Development slowly crept westward from the east coast, and eastward from the west, rubbing elbows at last with the most intractable stretches of the Everglades. The Florida Barge Canal, a proposed clear-cut canal across Florida, was started, but thankfully, eventually abandoned.

Many people in Florida, including me, live on what is probably reclaimed swampland. My daughter, the gardener, is always complaining about the poor quality of the soil. Nothing grows in fill dirt.

Living On the Edge

When you look at the map of Southeast Florida, and focus on Fort Lauderdale and its western suburbs, including Parkland, you see a green patch to the west. That is the Everglades. That is how close to the wild this school's location is. Being new, these western suburbs tend to be desirable. In fact, it appears from Parkland's website that they are still building new developments.

Newness. Suburbia. These are usually concepts we associate with safety.

Florida now has the dubious distinction of having had two mass shootings in the space of two years. The Pulse Nightclub shooting in 2016, was abhorrent enough, when seen from a distance. But close-up, it had special resonance for me.

My daughter was in Orlando that day, not far from the night club, just hours before the shooting occurred. When I heard about the shooting, I did not know if she was safe or not. A phone call later, and I learned she was already on her way home. I cannot claim to have had any significant worry that stemmed from the incident. But even experiencing a moment of that, a moment, spent contemplating the worst...

Yesterday's incident, taking place so close to what was once our home, and near to where many of our friends from that time still reside, strikes an even deeper chord. Perhaps because children—children the age of my high schoolers—children in a place we generally consider safe, a high school—were targeted. By a man who was barely more than a child himself.

Making Sense of Madness

I felt the same way after the San Bernardino shooting: the target was so inconceivable in its innocence—why shoot during a gathering for those with developmental disabilities? As if murder were rational. It is no more rational to plan a shooting based on religious extremism, racial prejudice, or homophobia. But because we have had previous experience with these terrible motives, we nod our heads and think we understand.

When we look at these incidents, we want to make sense of what we see. What are the factors at play? Hatred? Mental illness? Easily accessible weapons? A search for fame, or infamy? None of it makes any sense.

And we court danger by putting too much emphasis on any one factor. Each interest group seems to have their pet peeve. Gun control advocates seem to disregard the role of personal responsibility in the shootings. Those who would blame mental illness paint all the mentally ill with a broad brush. Mental illness does not, as a rule, beget violence. So, we fight about the probable cause and wave away the conversation, saying it is too soon, too soon. Too soon to speak of such things.

Columbine, Newtown, and now Parkland. Not a travel itinerary, but a roster of death. All of these neighborhoods and communities have been scarred, irretrievably, and now will be forever connected with a senseless killing. And in each town, children are the ones who paid the price.

Freedom Isn't Free

Floridians cannot be surprised at our inclusion in the ranks of communities that are suffering this kind of loss. We live in the land of the free, with a free market, and many personal freedoms. We freely move from one place to another within our state and nation. We are not required to show our "papers", nor do we have to enter or exit checkpoints and submit to a search.

Most of the time, this is a blessing, not a curse. But freedom isn't free, as they say.

Still, a child's life seems a bit too much to pay for any freedom. Much less seventeen lives.

River or Swamp?

In Florida, we have pushed forward and progressed, to ever greater, ever more comfortable, ever more convenient, and ever more numerous homes and businesses. We have cut taxes and made schools bear the brunt of it. We have chosen business over the sickly environment, and prosperity over the mental health needs of our children. We have turned our heads away and failed to act when action was required. Expecting nature and our children to somehow fend for themselves.

Schools, the province of our children, are not swampland to be cleared, so that a suburb may be built over it. We must treat our children, and the schools to which many of us entrust them, not as a worthless swamp, but as a treasured river. A river of grass, where each tiny blade, dancing in a sea of fresh water, is precious and essential. A natural resource which will ensure a bright future. Unless, of course, we fail to protect it from those who seek to plunder it.

May Congress, some day soon, heed its natural instinct to protect its own children, and thereby preserve in perpetuity, our most precious resource.

The Wardrobe of Kings Intro

4/14/2018

First published in April 2018, this poem was inspired by a book review in the *New York Times* discussing former FBI director James Comey's recent book about his experiences in government.

The poem is voiced, with great artistic license, from what I imagine to be Comey's point of view, as he addresses his boss, shortly before being fired.

It reminds us of the many people who have come and gone in the past four years, the vast majority of them, decent and dedicated public servants.

In this poem, I imagine Comey as some sort of white knight, trying to run his agency in an honorable way.

I hope you enjoy this playful interpretation of events. Events that are even now being re-interpreted as a *Showtime* movie.

The photograph I selected for my blogpost was of an Apostle Iris, since I referred to Comey as an apostle of order, of the Rule of Law. As in, a dedicated, loyal follower, not of a single person, but of principle.

Whether his actions actually live up to that title, is up to history to decide. He is blamed by many on the left, as the one who lost the election for Hilary Clinton by appearing before Congress on the issue of her emails, shortly before the election.

The "Wardrobe of Kings" refers to the FBI, which is the Federal "Bureau" of investigation, as in a chest of drawers or wardrobe. And of course, we all know a silly fairy tale, about the clothes that kings, or emperors, sometimes wear.

The Wardrobe of Kings

Apostle of order,
Knight-errant at law,
I have writ here
My final epistle:
I find you repellant.
I find you unethical,
To all of Earth,
Antithetical.

You clamber the cherry
Tree, picking the facts.
Dissembling is now
The new normal.
Every day I count six

Falsities or mis-leadings
That spew from your
Pursed lips, infernal.

Inspired by a robber
Who held me at gunpoint
In childhood, I soon
Was a squire,
Tasked with keeping the stronger
From maiming the weaker,
I guard independence
With law.

I saw much to appall me,
A show, playing nightly:
The boredom of torture
And capture,
While campaigns were a-waging
And pols were engaging
In duels, such gore
Bringing rapture.

Still, a soldier for Truth,
I squandered my youth
At the Bureau,
The wardrobe of kings.
I shield law from politics,
Fairly try heretics,
Ploddingly,
Wait in the wings,
While you twist and you stretch it—
I can't help but wretch—I
Recoil at the sight
Of such things.

Still, you speak to your circle,
So silent, assenting,
A mirror, deaf blind
To all else.
They're all longing to follow.
Your word is their mantra.
They insist that the rest
Must be false.

And now, what would you have of me?
Some oath of loyalty?
Kissing the ring
And conspiring?
I despair at your arrogance,
Slouching towards wickedness,
Torches ablaze at
Assizes.

I would gladly, gladly,
Galloping gallantly,
Lop off your crown
For the prizes,
Were it not for the litany
Of my own wickedry:
Was it not I
Who baptized you?

Statues Intro

7/31/2018

    This poem was written in July 2018 in response to a prompt from *What Pegman Saw*, a writing challenge based on different locations in the world each week.
    This poem is set in Kinshasa, which was once part of the Belgian Congo, Africa.
    It talks generally about statues portraying King Leopold of Belgium. You can see one such statue in an article in the *Flanders Today Newspaper*. The article discusses the controversy surrounding statues of King Leopold *inside* the country of Belgium.
    Congolese Belgians object to these statues, since they recall a horrible time in their history, during which many of their countrymen were killed. In the same vein, many in the US object to and have caused the dismantling of Confederate Statues in the US, especially since the Black Lives Matter protests have begun.

A more recent article gave the status of the issue in Belgium, as of June 2020. Another article about a statue of King Leopold *in Kinshasa* portrays quicker, more decisive action. This statue remained only while the Congo was still ruled by Belgium.

It was torn down and placed in a garbage heap in 1967, seven years after Independence had been regained.

In a tone-deaf move, this statue was once again returned to a prominent square in Kinshasa in 2005. It was supposed to be an educational reminder of the time, when the Congo was controlled by Belgium.

It lasted a mere 24 hours in that spot, before it was mysteriously removed.

This story reminds us of the power of symbols, both to exalt and to oppress, and the power of their destruction, both to condemn and to vindicate.

Statues

There was a king of long ago,
Who helped the sales of rubber go
Right through the roof. This royal sage
Helped usher in the industrial age.

And using kingly powers of old,
The Belgian Congo's Leopold,
A Western man, so full of pride,
Scarce blinked an eye, as millions died.

But this is now, and that was then.
Blood seeps into the ground, and when
We cannot see it, we forget.
Except the ones whose blood was let.

They live with us, and freely roam,

Who, once, were slaves in their own home.
They see nostalgic statuary
To men, to them, far worse than scary,

And yet, we recoil in surprise,
That History should offend their eyes!
So, too, Kinshasa, in grim reminder,
Re-erected him! Could they be blinder?

The statue lasted not a day.
The people locked the king away.

The Yoke Intro

8/5/2019

 The first line of this poem came from former President Obama's remarks on the tragic shootings that afflicted El Paso, Texas and Dayton, Ohio this week.
 I thought the expression "people of goodwill" sounded outdated and quaint enough to be poetic, and the rest flowed from it.
 This is my response to the stalling, that seems habitual these days in government, on this and many other issues.
 Of course, the citizenry is not blameless. Their passivity and apathy act as enabler to the government's inaction addiction.
 So here is my "call to arms," so to speak, to those sleepy citizens. Not just on the issue of the too easy availability of firearms, but on many other pressing, but more or less deliberately neglected matters of national and international importance.

The Yoke

People of goodwill,
Come take the journey,
Join the fight,

Though it be uphill.
Come lift the gurney
With all your might.

While the others jaw
And jab and bicker,
Strut and crow,

Lean into the saw.
This log is thicker
Than we know.

Though the powers that be
May own the present,
Cling to power,

Invincible are we.
The future's essence,
It is ours.

So be not faint of heart.
We've conquered demons,
Exorcized

Worse devils. We'll outsmart
These, bend their knees and
Minimize

Their stain. They'll, too, be long forgotten.
Never yet has Bad prevailed,
When honest people of goodwill
Put on the yoke of Good Travail.

Scrooge Intro

12/23/2019

    Here's a rather political poem for a rather political holiday season.
    In this poem, I re-count (and re-gift) some of the more unwelcome gifts our country has received in 2019, courtesy of one particular Scrooge, whose favorite color appears to be a very Christmas-y green.

Scrooge

Inserting uncertainty,
Masking the lie:
Disbelieve everything!
Question your eyes!

Insulting the serious,
Mocking the weak,
Caging the blameless,
Upstaging the meek;

Acting, reacting, and
Pivoting, fast,
Calling out, quibbling,
Ducking the ask;

Shooting the messenger,

Rolling your eyes,
Demanding detractors
Be cut down to size;

All the while, rolling in
Green, for the fight:
Merry Christmas to all,
And to all a good night!

On Pharaoh's Watch Intro

5/30/2020

In my busy life, with tasks never-ending, I have but a short supply of energy and a very small staff (namely me!) to do it all. Thinking about this, in the context of these hectic times, I immediately thought of the story of Joseph in Egypt, where he rises to become the Pharaoh's right-hand man, and has the great idea, to store grain in times of plenty, and dole it out, in times of famine.

Similarly, I must do what I must do a wee bit at a time. But having written the poem, I realize that this metaphor also describes government's basic function, to provide welfare to its citizens in times of need.

I imagine Joseph standing before some enormous ancient silo. He turns a spigot on, to pour out exactly one cup of grain. I imagine a long line of hungry Egyptians. And there, up high on a golden throne, is the Pharaoh, who looks something like Tutankhamen, in his blue and gold and spectacular eyeliner. Impassive. Barely deigning to look upon the unwashed.

I suspected that a spigot in ancient Egypt might be an anachronism. But per my googling, the spigot was invented around 1700 B.C. by the Romans, and Joseph is supposed to have lived, at right about the same time.

I picked a photo of a sun garden ornament for this blogpost because Re or Ra, the sun-god, was believed to be the divine father of the pharaohs. He was also the King of Gods and the patron of the pharaoh.

With our country going through multiple crises all at the same time, we really need the comfort and calming effect our leaders can have upon us, on those splendid occasions, when they do the right thing. We need them to assure us that everything will be okay. That they have it under control. That they support the experts and are staying out of the experts' way.

Now is the time for leaders to concern themselves with the welfare of their citizens. Not with their own greed or vanity. Whether that means staying out of the way, coming up with creative new solutions, speaking out, or staying silent.

Let us hope that instead of acting on their own perverse whims, our leaders will be divinely inspired, to do what is right.

To hear the poem as intended, speak the first line of each stanza slowly, and read the rest at a normal pace.

On Pharaoh's Watch

I am Joseph,
Sharing grain
With all the nation.
Pharaoh watching,
Motionless,
Upon his golden perch.

Don't pour grain,
During famine,
Willy-nilly.
Measure out
A single cup,
A single family's worth.

Grain, like gold,
Fills the storehouse,
Times of plenty.
Seven years, a
Golden stream,
Like interest, on a coin.

Famine hits,
And the lines,
They wind and wiggle.
Hungry people
Shuffle bowls,
Not knowing where they're going.

Seven years,
We have feasted
At the table,
Chugging from
the fountain,
Gorging from the golden trough.

Now we grieve,
Suffer pain,
Humiliation.
Pharaoh's eyelid twitches...
Reaches.
Turns the spigot off.

Dominate Intro

6/4/2020

The events of this past week in Minneapolis, where I spent part of my childhood, have been very upsetting and disturbing to me.

First, the horrible acts in the video we all saw, from many angles: In the course of an arrest for a petty crime, a white policeman, aided by his fellow officers, kneeled on the neck of a black man, long enough to end his life.

Second, the protests, which have spread like wildfire across this nation. These protests affirm the value of all black lives, especially those unjustifiably ended, at the hands of the police. Though unusual, in a largely apathetic and politically passive nation, these protests show that people are sick of the same old, same old.

That encourages me. There is a caring populace, willing to at least raise their voices and march in the streets, to demand reasonable and long-awaited change. At the same time, I worry about the opportunists, the looters and the fire-setters, who deflate the credibility of the peaceful protesters, and play into the hands of those who oppose them and try to crush them, like sitting ducks.

I wrote this poem in response to what happened in Lafayette Square Park, across from the White House, in Washington, D.C. on June 2, 2020. The events, in case you are unfamiliar, are these: Protesters filled the park during daylight hours. Then US Attorney General William Barr toured the park with a security detail. Then a group of policemen on horses batonned and tear-gassed the protesters out of the park. Then, with an entourage of various officials and cameramen, the President toured the empty park, surveying the damage from the previous night's fires, and finally, walked across the street to St John's Episcopal church, for a pious and self-serving photo-op with a Bible.

All of this time, the airwaves and Twittersphere have been splattered with the venom of the President's threat, of military force against his own people. This, I find most disturbing of all. It calls to mind the charging armed horsemen under Charles I of England during the English Civil War, or Czar Alexander's show of force against peasant protesters, immediately before the Russian revolution. Lots of movies and documentaries (*Dr. Zhivago* comes to mind) recount such scenes. And we find them especially powerful, because we know that they could never happen here.

Dominate

Dominate the battlespace,
Once said the military.
No matter, that the space is here,
And we, the Enemy.

Dominate the battlespace.
Don't give an inch, not ever.
No matter, that you spill our blood,
To earn your victory.

And look! Your owly sidekick
Walks the crowded park, before you.
He notes the many obstacles.
And writes them in his book:

The mothers, pushing strollers

Past the chanters, of all backgrounds,
Who bow and kneel and raise their fists,
With anger in their look.

In camera-friendly daylight,
Cavaliers are swiftly riding,
Like czarist troops, on horseback,
In this age of cars and planes.

Anachronistic? Maybe,
But no less effective, for it.
Their rubber bullets, tear gas,
Strong batons shall dominate.

Voila! The park is empty!
Picture-perfect for a selfie:
Your proof, you dared to leave the bunker,
Take a Tuesday stroll.

Observe the burnt-out restroom.
Shake your head, in solemn sorrow.
A sudden urge comes on, to pray:
Across the street you go.

St John's is waiting for you,
Sanctuary to the nation.
Its pews held bygone presidents,
Whose tears, their prayers drowned.

Our sacred space, and yours, collide.
But what's this, in your pocket?
We watch you pose, your Holy Book,
So fresh, un-opened, upside-down.

It's not enough, you dominate

ANDREA W LEDEW

Our airwaves, conversation.
Absurd distractions mock us.
Every act, our mourning, slights.

Don't bother, guessing motives.
We'll archive this falsest moment,
Like Bush's cruiser "triumph", or
The "V" of Nixon's flight.

A law-and-order president?
Defending, minimizing,
Such actions, indefensible?
Such crimes, you cannot hide.

Look out! The camera's rolling,
Every cell phone trained upon you.
As clouds of tear gas melt away,
The tears roll from our eyes.

Suddenly Silent Intro

7/11/2020

The news this week is not all virus-related.

A number of Supreme Court decisions were announced. Our majority-conservative Court proved itself up to the task, impressing even moderates and liberals.

The case determining that the Presidency has to obey a subpoena for documents, rather than ignoring it, had the news networks crowing, The Rule of Law has been vindicated!

At the same time, prosecutors on Presidential cases are being pressured to leave their positions.

It made me think about how law infiltrates our lives, and, like music, is appreciated most, in its absence.

I pictured a violin string in the first stanza, and the orchestra grew from there. I could not find a violin image. So, I settled for a thing of beauty.

Suddenly Silent

The law's a thing of beauty.
The law's a silver string.
So few attempt to play it.
So few can make it sing.

Its body, carved by ancients,
Who pulled it taut and lean;
Its breath, a whisp of horsehair;
Its pull and push, serene.

We learn at Father's footstool.
We learn at Mother's knee.
We learn the tune of justice,
The tone, of liberty.

We hum it with our heartstrings.
We drum it on our bones.
We trumpet it from rooftops.
Our bells, its spells intone.

Harmonious and happy,
Or dissonant and dull,
We revel in vibrations.
We tremble, at its lull.

The rule of law, presiding,
Conducts this symphony.
In such a sudden silence, what
Becomes of you and me?

Smoky Intro

9/14/2020

    In this poem, I draw on the tragedy of the Fall 2020 wildfires out West for my metaphor. Which, as it happens, applies just as well to someone in the East.

Smoky

Shouting "Fire!" at the movies;
Puppeteer-ed by a Russian Troll;
Preaching "Everything is groovy!"
Sinking deeper, in a hole;
Making a splash at maskless rallies,
Though you're King of the Masquerade;
Captured by your fibs fantastic;
Forced to lie in the bed you made;
Topic of many a virulent sonnet;
Making the bane of your name profane;
Stoking the pyre, while perched upon it:
Mocking the West Coast, all a-flame:
Claim that you aren't to blame, you liar!
Where there's smoke, there's fire.

Debatable Intro

10/8/2020

    I said in my last post that this is not the time for satire. But if you can't laugh now, how can you cope?
    I used the image of a broken window in my blogpost to illustrate my point. A broken window no longer functions as a window. If I describe what I am selling to you, sight unseen, as a window, would you expect that window to arrive broken? Or would you think that my glowing sales pitch had left out a few crucial details?
    This rhyme makes fun of a similar alternative reality, being presented to the American People as Fact.
    In the famous Spanish novel by Cervantes, *Don Quixote*, Sancho Panza is Don Quixote's ever-present loyal follower and sidekick. He serves as a contortionist-style apologist, or explainer-in-chief, of his boss's deluded ravings.

Many details of the poem are pulled from current events. The Boat Parade refers to one held in Trump's honor, here in Jacksonville, Florida.

The *superlative*, for those who are not up on their grammar, is the form of the adjective that takes the ending -est (good, better, *best*; silly, sillier, *silliest*.)

I hope you will agree that using the adjective "superlative" is no exaggeration, when one is describing the Exaggerator-In-Chief.

Debatable

I trounced the Left in my debate,
Succeeding there, to dominate
The frail and weak, the old and lame,
The codger, Liberal, What's-His-Name.

My sidekick Sancho had his day
And blew that Communist away,
With soporific sighs, sublime,
And masculinely, stole her time.

Oh, do not fear dear COVID's kiss!
For only wusses die from this.
No heroes let themselves be caged!
Such play is for a children's stage.

When I felt fluish, I departed

In a chopper (which was smart!)
And spent a day or two away,
With docs, who signed an NDA.

And while a-bed, a cocktail took—
A Cure! And now, I feel and look
Like me, some twenty years ago!
God blessed me, with a miracle!

Why should I fret? Though twenty-eight
Now quarantine, I'm feeling great!
And do not feel a bit contagious.
Though I find it quite outrageous

That a drive, to see my fans
(Quite pumped, with steroids in my veins)
Should be critiqued! Opposable?
Aren't bodyguards disposable?

I'll never get a passing grade
From polls: Fake News.
But Boat Parade?

All Made Up Intro

10/17/2020

    This poem talks of cakes and circus clowns, but its mood is anything but celebratory. I am sure there are those out there besides me, longing for truth, in this age of prevarication, and bait and switch. If only we knew what lay underneath all that frosting.

All Made Up

Poetry's the mortar
That we spread upon our lives
To cover up the interstitial cracks.

Poetry's the frosting
On those sweet, delicious moments,
The binder that disguises ugly facts.

Slather on foundation,
Like a second skin of falseness,
Pick your pretty words to calm the din,

Smiling, like a circus clown,
Parade around in make-up,
Disguising what a world of hurt we're in.

Electoral Intro

12/14/2020

On this day, when the electoral college voted at last, and gave us an official President Elect, we had other news as well.

A new vaccine punctured the arms of health workers across the country, even while the death toll from COVID-19 hit the 300,000 mark. Our attorney general resigned. And still the lawsuits continue, and dust is still being kicked up somewhere, in the name of some legal theory or another.

One can't even begin to make coherent sentences to describe it.

The arcane electoral college, which almost no one understands, aligned somehow with the popular vote, just as Jupiter aligns with Mars, in *The Age of Aquarius*. Science pricked a pinhole of light in the darkness of this pandemic with its hypodermic needle. And even the greatest of loyalists have fallen to the wayside, to avoid being torn asunder by the teeth of the Constitution's relentless machinery.

All is working well. Yet all is not well, as we watch the COVID numbers climb a vertical wall, with no summit in sight.

In this nonsensical time, nonsense is said, and nonsense is believed.

Electoral

Byzantine.
Libertine.
New vaccine.
Resignation.

Electoral.
Quite amoral.
Un-pastoral.
Accreditation.

Learn the law.
Tooth and claw.
Spin and yaw.
Dull tradition.

Long in tooth.

Old, forsooth!
Dodge the truth.
Plot sedition.

Lie, confuse.
Cheat, abuse.
Fast and loose.
Late the hour.

Write the check.
Wring the neck.
What the heck--
Cling to power.

Great Patriots Intro

1/7/21

    Like many Americans, I saw the events of last night unfold on live TV. Watching, aghast, from my comfortable couch.
    While the electoral votes were in the process of being certified by Congress, while the ridiculous question of whether they should be certified was being debated, Trump supporters, who were gathered outside, suddenly mounted the steps of the Capitol Building with only anemic opposition.
    They broke their way inside, wandering the halls and ransacking offices for a while, carrying flags and even the Confederate Flag through our State building. They sent our elected officials scurrying for cover, underground.
    It was hours before order was restored, and the current President played virtually no part. That is, until he was shamed on national TV into saying something, by his replacement, Biden. Even then, the President's message was half congratulation, and half, polite request to move along.

Yet another reality-TV season-ending drama, as my husband so aptly put it. It reminded me of the feel-good seventies' pop psychology books which predicted that if you like comedies, your life will play out like a comedy. If you like dramas or soap operas, your life will play out like a drama or soap opera.

Well, if you like reality TV...

I feel shame and embarrassment at this moment, and worry, about our reputation in the world. I searched for posts on Twitter by German newspapers and magazines and came upon two from *der Spiegel*. One of them showed some of the 28 covers of the magazine (so far) featuring our president in less than flattering ways. Another was an editorial by the Secretary of State of Germany, with the first line, roughly translated, saying:

> The pictures from the storming of the Capitol pain the soul of every friend of democracy.
> Heiko Maas (SPD), Bundesaussenminister

This poem came to me as a rant, voiced by one of the participants. Please read, knowing this voice is *not mine*. Let us be gentler with our democracy/republic in the future, and may the world pardon what, with any luck, is the last gasp of this administration.

A few notes on references: *Great Patriots* is the term Trump used to refer to his supporters who stormed the Capitol Building, addressing them in a tweet. I consider this a dog whistle.

The image of the cowboy boot prints on the beach comes from a great photo I saw on the blog of *priorhouse*. It seemed to me to belong to a person who is comfortable going against the stream, who is not afraid of being different, and who is proud of their identity, regardless of what people think.

The line *let the first be last* is of course, from the Bible:

So the last shall be first, and the first last: for many be called, but few chosen.

       Matthew 20:16 King James Version

The image of a dog jumping for treats refers to promises made by politicians, now and in the past, but never delivered on.

It also brings to mind a statistic I picked up from the Jon Meecham documentary, *The Soul of America*. The historian closes the documentary saying, that the price of living as the middle class did in the post WWII years in the US was $130,000 in today's dollars. Whereas the current average income here today is $56,000.

Which leads me to believe there may be some merit in this frightening show of discontent.

Great Patriots

Cowboy boot prints on the beach.
Rage against the storm.
Jump, for treats just out of reach.
Clash against reform.
Hail a flag of Southern Pride.
Wallow in the past.
Spurn Elites, the smart, deride.
Let the first be last.

Storm the Bastille! Climb the gates!
The barricades stampede!
Vault the steps and crash the glass!
For nothing shall impede
The cause of Freedom, Liberty,
The Fight to Stop the Steal!
And all the world shall feel our pain,

ANDREA W LEDEW

Our basest shame, revealed.

They do not understand us, and
They do not care to know!
How useless, this "Democracy,"
To fight so vile a foe!
We flaunt our grassroots legacy,
Our loyalty, pristine.
All Hail, Man of the People!
(Though you're absent from the scene.)

They cannot know what's good for them,
This vapid, voting fray!
Americans did not mean
What they said, Election Day!
We want a new Do-Over, and
If that's not in the cards,
We'll gladly take autocracy,
If Our Man is in charge.

A red hat for Abe Lincoln.
Leaders cowering from our screams.
And all the world is watching us.
What next? The guillotines?

Interregnum Intro

1/12/21

Interregnum, the time between regimes, translates from Latin to something like "between kings." In either case, a fitting name for our times.

Fire-ants, for those not familiar, are a breed of small red ants common in Florida, that do not take kindly to having their ant piles stepped upon. They will quickly punish the clumsy foot that commits such a heinous crime. Mostly they are just irritating and make your feet itch. But for some, too many ant bites, I am told, can result in a terrible life-threatening allergic reaction.

May this current mayhem be but a tiny irritating sting, in the otherwise robust health of this vibrant country.

Interregnum

Plywood on the White House.
Cobwebbed, shattered glass.
Fences round the High Court.
Banners in the grass.

Swarming, just like fire-ants,
Descending on their prey.
Engulf our errant footsteps.
Let Chaos reign, today.

A sickness in the Chamber,
is hiding, without masks.
What need have we for bullets when
A virus does the task?

Incompetents, neglectful:

What harm can come from these?
Oh, yes--Five people lost their lives,
And thousands spread disease.

Meanwhile, Inaugurators
Erect a wooden stage,
Like wooden gallows found within
This crowd of vice and rage.

Some clamor for impeachment,
Demand the Twenty-Fifth,
While rabid rumors on the net
Meet corporate censorship.

What happened to the country
Our fathers recognized?
This monumental battlefield
Brings sorrow to their eyes.

Q & A Intro

1/14/21

Most every blog has a Q & A, or question and answer page, but this one may be a little different from some you've seen.

The letter "Q" has come to mean some pretty strange things in recent days, most prominent among them, Qanon. I am trying to answer its use as a rabble-rouser, with the "A" being our reaction, as responsible citizens of all stripes, to condemn criminal misbehavior, to stop the divisiveness that has led to it, and to just get along with each other, already.

I suppose that makes me profoundly naïve. But writing a poem, focused on the letter Q and its *Doppelgänger* A, was an interesting exercise, nonetheless.

To readers on both sides of the aisle, if you must step over the line, make sure it is the line in the *center* of the aisle. And make sure your hand is outstretched in friendship, when you do so.

The picture used with this poem on my website recalls the fires set during the protests in the summer of 2020. These were happily absent, though they were replaced by even more disturbing events, during this most recent uprising at the Capitol. The photo also symbolizes my wish that in the future, everyone will get along like a house on fire.

Q & A

Questioning the basest
Quotidian details.
Questing for meaning,
For Quality hacks.

Querulous chasing,
Like Quadrupeds, racing,
Quelling your rage with
Conspiracies, Quacks.

Quantities milling, round
Quorum-bound hostages,
Quarrel about killing,
Then Quickly agree.

You'll Answer your Actions,

Our Agile response is.
Admit human failing.
Adapt, and be free.

Accessible, Always,
Your Anger's subsiding.
You're Aghast at your Actions!
You were Addled, online.

Show Aptitude! Work
In Alliance, together!
Combine our Abilities.
Anchor the line.

Audit our processes.
Aim to be better.
Act as a country,
As women and men!

Access your empathy.
Join All together.
Making Amends,
Be united, Again.

Waste Intro

2/2/21

    This poem takes a historical approach, describing how different periods of time have collected and then discarded different things.

Waste

Each age has its own.

Open sewers running free.
Smoke-choked skies and shipwrecked seas.
Each age has its own.

Letters piled up to the sky.
Newspapers, a million high.
Each age has its own.

Silent music never played.
Lost to time, the movies fade.
Each age has its own.

Sludgy lakes and poisoned ponds.
Smoggy cities. Species, gone.

ANDREA W LEDEW

Each age has its own.

Photos, precious: digitized.
Bits and bytes, metastasized.
Each age has its own.

Brittle bottles on the beach.
Changing course seems out of reach.
Each age has its own.

Corpses, corpses, piling high.
Bill of Rights hung out to dry.
Each age has its own.

The Mighty Intro

In Memory of Brian Sicknick, Capitol Police

2/3/2021

    I wrote this poem while watching on TV the memorial service at the Capitol, where Brian Sicknick lay in state. He was apparently one of the few civilians ever to be afforded that honor. Brian Sicknick was a Capitol Policeman, charged with guarding the Capitol building, and was injured when he was attacked by rioters on January 6. He died the next day of his injuries.
    I found the rhythmic, synchronized motions of the policemen who celebrated his life very moving, and their solemnity really brought home what a blow it is to us all, to lose a guardian of our liberty in such a way. My sympathies to the family and I hope they will excuse me for trespassing on their grief, with my poem.

The Mighty

Below the dome, the velvet ropes
Encircle. Placed with care,
The ashes, oh, the ashes join
The flag's enfolding stare.

The cops approach them, two by two.
The sentries never flinch,
Then march the relics down the staircase,
Inch by solemn inch.

A cold day, at the Capitol.
The bagpipes wheeze like wind.
The Speaker's hair blows to and fro.
Her legs are stockinged, thin.

The cops line up like soldiers

And they bow their heads in prayer.
Their white gloves rise in one salute,
And rend the frigid air.

The bike cops push off jointly,
As their bomber blues inflate,
Then motorbikes with sidecars
Guide the hearse, as black as slate.

To Arlington, to Arlington!
What potentate or king?
What senator, what governor
Lies centered in this ring?

What mighty man has earned such laurels?
Hero, to us all.
He gave his life to guard this fortress.
How the Mighty fall.

Round Two Intro

2/12/2021

>Those who can make you believe absurdities can make you commit atrocities.
>Voltaire, quoted by Senator James Raskin (Maryland), Impeachment Manager

    I wrote this poem as the House Democrats' case for Impeachment, Round Two, drew to a close.
    You may recall that President Trump was impeached once before, in early 2019, for calling the President of Ukraine and threatening to withhold funding, if the President of Ukraine did not deliver evidence of Hunter

Biden's supposed misdeeds in that country. Trump intended to smear his likely rival for the Presidency—and now the President— Hunter Biden's father Joe Biden, with that information. The Ukrainian President knew better than to cooperate. Perhaps because the arrangement was never fully brought to fruition, only attempted, the charges against Trump did not stick and he was acquitted by a Senate controlled by his own party.

This time around, like many other onlookers, I was weirdly drawn to the vulgarity-laced video of January 6th's mayhem. It was shown chronologically, alongside the President's provocations and responses, or lack of response. I was troubled and impressed by the participants' strength of conviction, their seeming sincerity of purpose, however misguided.

Many of them are now in jail.

Their inspiration, meanwhile, has time to go golfing.

On January 6, the National Guard did eventually come, no thanks to the former president, and the crowd was disbursed and the building cleared. So, the insurrection, as the House managers so archaically call it, was just an attempt to take over a government building, a bungled attempt. As a mere attempt, I fear it is going to go the way of the last Impeachment--no harm, no foul.

Our beloved institutions and time-honored processes were intended and constructed to work well. I believe they are sound and will likely serve us for many years to come.

It just seems that lately, they have proven no match for the determined manipulations of unscrupulous people. No match, for the self-echoing partisanship of a fifty-fifty nation.

But there is hope. It could be, that by their votes, the men (and women) of the Senate will choose to serve their country, rather than their ambition.

Round Two

These sacred walls.
These hallowed halls.
This solemn, marbled chamber.
These velvet chairs.
These well-worn stairs.
And not a hint of danger.

This floor, where hate
Becomes debate,
And logjams, compromises.
This gallery
Of valor rings
The valley of the wisest.

Now once again,
Elected men

Their arguments impart,
That weaponed words,
Though most absurd,
Have torn our world apart.

They came here first
For rival's dirt
Extracted with a truncheon.
Against the law?
Not so! Guffaw!
A minor lapse of judgment.

But now, He chose
To rend His clothes,
To claim His victory stolen.
And they, like sheep,
His lies believed,
Stampeding chambers holy.

While some stood tall,
And voted, all,
His rival to anoint,
His faulty facts
Provoked attacks
Upon the chambers joint.

They prosecute and
They salute,
With video montage,
His deeds and words,
The pleas, unheard:
Cacophonous collage.

But when they vote,
What part will dote

ANDREA W LEDEW

On, grease His fragile ego?
What circus games!
What lion taming!
Look! A crime is legal!

What fault's to find?
Who dares opine
A slur, against this brute?
Such calumny
Could primary
Your seat! You'd get the boot!

Is this high crime?
Will He do time?
Well, this I highly doubt.
For party-line prevails.
Stop whining!
Vote the bastards out!

Minor Edits Intro

3/12/21

March 11, 2021 was the one-year anniversary of the date when the World Health Organization declared COVID-19 a pandemic.

I woke up, bleary-eyed, to the news.

Mitch McConnell, the Republican leader of the US Senate, had made the following statement.

> For weeks, every indicator has suggested our economy poised to come roaring back, with more job openings for Americans who need work. None of these trends began on Jan. 20. President Biden and his Democratic government inherited a tide that had already begun to turn toward decisive victory. In 2020, Congress passed five historic bipartisan bills to save our

health system, protect our economic foundations, and fund Operation Warp Speed to find vaccines. Senate Republicans led the bipartisan CARES Act that got our country through the last year.

Mitch McConell

The statement on its face seems pretty irrefutable.

So many unsung heroes have been trying to fight this virus and reverse its economic effects all year. So many politicians, Republican and Democrat, have cast their votes to help those in need. The programs, that Democrats neglect to give Republicans credit for, helped prevent worse outcomes from happening.

Offended by the Democrats taking a victory lap, McConnell seems to imply that Republicans should get the bulk of the credit. They got the ball rolling, after all.

But McConnell mentioned only those things that reflected positively on the past administration and those loyalists in its orbit. Without mentioning how, over the past year, these very same heroes stood in their own way, and prevented the nation from getting here sooner.

That time wasted has cost us lives.

There's plenty of praise and blame to go around. But I agree with McConnell. We should look at the full, un-edited record before we assign credit.

Minor Edits

Remember, remember,
A year in the making,
A year, full of faking
And farcical jeers;

Remember, remember,
The strutting and booing,
The pompous poo-pooing
That got us all here;

Look at the ball
That you all set in motion.
With unproven potions,
De minimus rants.

Look at poor Sisyphus,

Pushing it up:
Overnight, it falls back
To the bottom, again.

Remember, remember,
Court jesters, court-tasters,
The babbling timewasters,
Publicity stunts;

Remember, remember,
The speakers of truth,
The victims of ruthless
Blows, insults, and grunts.

Now, now, that it's over,
This yearful of turmoil,
Of protests and snake oil,
Alternative facts,

Don't give me this earful:
You should take the credit?
All year, you've been editing
Us.
With an axe.

A Vote Intro

Senator Raphael Warnock's First Senate Floor Address, March 17, 2021

3/18/2021

Yesterday the news--at least the news I watch--was full of the new Senator from Georgia. The Reverend Raphael Warnock made his maiden speech to the Senate floor. And it was a doozy.

The speech took place on a busy news day:
- A possible hate crime had taken place, killing eight Asian women in Warnock's home state.

- A surge of 250 post-insurrection voter-suppression bills were being proposed in most of the individual states.

- A massive voting rights bill (*The For the People Act*) was being set into motion by the majority Democrats.

Warnock used his maiden address to speak in support of that bill. The bill seeks to outlaw the aforementioned efforts at voter suppression.

According to Warnock, these efforts and their predecessors have only been allowed to crop up, because of the current legislative vacuum. A vacuum which has existed, ever since the Supreme Court asked the legislature to fix the Voting Rights Act of 1965. Eight years ago.

The common wisdom is that this new Voting Rights legislation doesn't have a "hope" of passage, in our divided and filibuster-ized Senate.

Enter stage left, Senator Warnock.

Senator Warnock said, "A vote is a kind of prayer." This phrase seemed to echo, in both word order and meter, the first line of Emily Dickinson's classic poem, *"Hope" is the thing with feathers*.

In my own poem, I mimic her style. I also try to capture her sense of awe and reverence for an undervalued thing. The poem seeks to convince us that this thing should, nonetheless, be precious to us all.

In the course of this exercise, I came to realize, just how close the concept of Hope is, to the act of Voting. They are, in fact, intertwined.

If you do have twenty minutes or so, I recommend a listen to *Sen Warnock's speech*. As for myself, I look forward to more of the same.

May his fellow Senators feel just as inspired. And cast their own votes, upholding voting rights for all.

A Vote

A "vote" is a kind of prayer--
A tiny cry for help--
A whispered wish upon the wind--
A statement of the self--

It signals stronger spirits--
The Great must hear our cry--
It sets alarm bells ringing--
With smoke that rises high--

Though eyes may wince from wishing--
And no one dares to talk--
But still, we place our silent hopes
Into that silent box.

Why strip us of our wishes?

Why silence silent prayer?
A man who'd countenance such things--
Has got no business there.

Liberal Wish List Intro

4/13/2021

    I wrote this poem upon reading that the infrastructure bill had been mockingly referred to as a "Liberal wish-list" by Senate Republican Leader Mitch McConnell, in a page from the Senate Republican Leader's own office. This is not the first time he has used this turn of phrase. Googling the term, I found he had used it to refer to the coronavirus relief package earlier this year and had even used it as far back as the Obama stimulus package, in 2010.

    I wonder, what would Liberals themselves put at the top of their list, if they knew that Republicans would actually read it? You may call me Pollyanna, but here's what would be on my Liberal Wish-List:

Liberal Wish List

I wish there was not an "L" word.
I wish we could get along.
I wish we could get past talking points.
I wish we could all belong.
I wish we could feed the hungry.
I wish we could get rich, too.
I wish we could live as neighbors.
I wish for a smile from you.
I wish that I understood you.
I wish I could call you friend.
I wish we could work together,
And compromise, stretch, and bend.
For all of my wistful wishing,
No matter the circumstance,

Whatever is on my wish list,
You're certain to vote against.

Public Servant Intro

5/13/2021

This poem is about our attitudes toward those who work for the government, and how these attitudes have changed since the mid-twentieth century. Like everything else in life, the trend seems to be, to careen toward the extremes. Entropy, I guess.

But this loudly proclaimed assumption--that government workers are incompetent and full of mercenary intent--affects humble workers, who are just trying to do their jobs well, far from the limelight. In addition, polluting the air with politics may eventually require public servants to sign on to something like a statement of faith. Such demands for political purity are reprehensible. And often self-defeating.

To me, this devolution of trust and respect toward government plays a role in many current events, from Senator Liz Cheney's ouster from her leadership position, to the bizarre phenomenon of vaccine hesitancy, to the passion of BLM protestors, in response to police brutality.

Our lack of trust in government may be grounded in both fact and history. But that makes it no easier for government workers to do their jobs.

Assuming, instead, that they deserve a basic level of trust and respect, would probably prove more productive, in the long run, than hurling insults --if not projectiles-- their way.

A government, trying to operate without the trust of the public, is a government hobbled on one foot.

Public Servant

We're professionals.
We're experts in our field.
We command your full respect.
To learned reason, you must yield.

We are there to serve.
But not, to be abused.
Others hold the reins of power.
We just walk the way they choose.

We are there to push
The paper off our desks,
Implement decisions made,
Do our jobs, as we know best.

We are guns for hire,

The puppets of The Man.
Our purpose is to swindle you,
To steal your stuff, as best we can.

We're the Enemy.
We cannot be trusted.
The whole Machinery of State
Is broken down and busted.

Some beg, to disagree,
And so, must be expelled.
The penalty of doing right:
To lose the right, to do it well.

Public Square Intro

5/27/2021

Perhaps I have watched too many episodes of *Murdoch*, a detective series set in the 1890s and early 1900's. But I find myself yearning for a nineteenth-century point of view, where, I imagine, there would be no confusing good and bad, or wrong and right.

In my high school days, we spoke with reverence about the great debates of American history. I remember marveling to learn, that once, long before the microphone, a general education emphasized oratorical skills and logic. Skills, which are often sorely lacking in the public discourse of today.

In law school First Amendment discussions, we spent a great deal of time talking about the Public Forum. This location, like the Roman or Greek forum, was supposed to be a place, where free speech was allowed and debate proceeded, unfettered.

The public forum seems to have morphed, over time, from the Roman forum or colonial town square, to the hustings and soapboxes of the nineteenth century, to various private places, like shopping malls, in the twentieth, to the very devices we carry around in our pockets, today.

At the same time, we have gradually shortened our attention spans. We tire easily of political speeches and prefer the gratification of splashy entertainment and the split-second flash of something new on our feed.

The content of our debate seems to have changed over time, as well. More and more people consider their opinions worth sharing, without regard to age, education, or expertise on any given topic. And--at the risk of sounding like a snob-- also without regard to whether the topic itself is worthy of discussion. Having too many voices makes it that much harder to find the real experts in the bunch.

I'm afraid all this historical pondering has led me to use obscure, archaic vocabulary in my poem. For which I heartily apologize.

Public Square

Complaint is the currency of our age,
The ticket to the Great Debate--
Or podium. Young buck, or sage,
Each struggles, to ingratiate

His listening public, fandom, with
His own uniqueness, point of view,
And others listen, gauge his pith,
Remix a version of his brew.

And so, the cycle goes, and we,
Who stand aside and hardly speak,
Are quite confounded, secretly.
They wail. We would not make a peep.

Some still recall the Public Square,

Once grand and mighty, full of men
Debating, till they gasped for air,
With elocution, gravamen,

On politics, morality,
On what is art and what is not,
On Life, in its totality,
Why we deserve the things we've got.

Look how reduced, the Public Square!
But little pixels on a screen!
No wonder, that they fill the air
With idle gossip, vented spleen.

For while they spin their precious tales,
So self-absorbed, delirious,
We shake our heads and wonder why
TV seems almost serious.

Where are those voices that can lead,
That dare, "Eureka!" to declare?
Drowned out, I fear, by all this screed.
So, rest in peace, the Public Square.

The Racket Intro

6/3/2021

    This poem complains about the constant noise of modern life, and the incessant and often trivial demands for our attention. Sometimes, we just need to turn it all off.

    Wishing you relief, in this time of noise and bluster!

    For those who don't know, Walter Cronkite was a news anchor on CBS in the seventies when I was growing up. Half an hour with him was enough to make you feel you understood what was happening in the world. Although most people made sure to read the paper as well! Even in the midst of Watergate, the Vietnam War, kidnappings, hijackings, protests and uprisings of all sorts, his voice made you feel like everything was going to be all right.

The Racket

Passwords. Emails. Insurrections.
Voices whimpering: internet.
Voices shouting: television.
Is the racket over yet?

Advertisements want my eyeballs.
Blogs insist I stay onscreen.
Threats of imminent destruction.
Faulty voting on machines.

Lord, where is that voice I trusted?
Walter Cronkite, rise again!
Tell me, should I be disgusted?
What is happening? Where and when?

Facts and facts and yet more facts

Should shape my gaping-open mind.
Yet what I see is parallax:
My lens distorts the view I find.

Escaping screens, I sit at nightfall
On the porch. The darkness thickens.
Summer breeze wafts over all.
Silence. All I hear is crickets.

Burning Flags Intro

7/8/2021

I remember long ago reading about a case, where a man burnt an American flag in protest. It took place outside Dallas City Hall, during Reagan's Republican National Convention in 1984. The man was arrested for desecrating the American flag and appealed his case up to the Supreme Court.

The case was *Texas vs. Gregory Lee Johnson*, 491 US 397 (1989.) It decided that flag burning was protected speech, under the First Amendment of the US Constitution. It overturned the laws that outlawed any desecration of the American flag. Laws that were in effect in 48 of the 50 states at the time. It stated that the government could not prohibit "expression of an idea simply because society finds the idea itself offensive or disagreeable."

The recent controversy over certain subjects being taught in school, such as "critical race theory," seems to me to be the same sort of patriotic tempest in a teapot.

An interesting July 7, 2021 Facebook post by *Heather Cox Richardson*, a political historian, talks about a recent book reading. The book was called "*Forget the Alamo,*" an obvious play on words, defying the resounding patriotism of "Remember the Alamo!" a slogan taught as history, to children of my vintage.

She notes how people reacted with outrage, to a narrative that, in academic circles, had long been considered established history. I guess it offended their sensibilities, because it contradicted what they had been taught as children. Heaven forbid, that what we teach as History should ever change. In this instance, the *book reading was cancelled* because it was deemed too upsetting. Also in Texas, as it happens.

In the Facebook post she goes on to explain that subjects which provoke this kind of outrage now have a name: "divisive." Bills have been drafted to combat this kind of subversive attack on our traditional patriotic values. I found Florida's, which was introduced in April. Think tanks are behind the language. They provide pre-packaged versions of this legislation, and so many others. All the legislator has to do is introduce it and pass it. I'm not sure if ours was passed or not, but I do know that school rules were changed to achieve similar ends. And a local schoolteacher was held up to ridicule, for openly supporting Black Lives Matter.

The parallels between flag burning and outlawing subjects of discussion in school seem ripe, for poetry.

Burning Flags

Legislatures
Make the law,
Or so their Latin
Roots imply.

Instigators
Sink their claws,
And write their copy,
On the sly.

Copycats,
In fancy three-piece
Suits, ideas
Introduce,

Word-for-word

From think-tank cronies,
Offering red meat,
To seduce.

Burning flags
Is not a passion
Many have,
That I have known.

Yet, this powder
Keg upon
The burning pyre
Is always thrown.

So, "divisive"
Topics may
No longer grace
The hallowed halls

Of schools, where they
Might cause a stir,
Provoke disgrace,
And shame us all.

Burning flags,
At rallies
Most political,
Were silent Speech.

Teaching race, or
Sex, or class, implies
The teacher's
Free to teach.

What's the harm,

In either practice?
We've forgotten
History.

Our foundation's
Built on broken
Shards of false
Idolatry.

Foul Ball Intro

7/15/2021

    I was appalled, yet somehow inspired--"shocked, but not surprised" as I so often hear people say, without any sense of self-contradiction-- by a news item this morning. The news said that Rudy Giuliani, the former President's attorney, came up with the idea of *losing the election, but then saying that they won.*
    This idea proved quite popular. And a perfectly good election has been given the third degree, as a result.
    During this month of empty-standed Tokyo Olympics games, it occurred to me that this lack of sportsmanship would never fly, in any other sport. Only in politics.
    This poem ensued. For anyone not familiar with baseball, I'm so sorry. I don't think I could explain it, if I tried.

Foul Ball

The pitcher winds up,
Plants his feet,
And rises,
Like a cartwheel.

The ball, it whizzes
To the plate.
The batter waits,
A spring,

All coiled and ready.
Strikes the ball,
And hits it
With a venom,

Releasing it,

To catapult
Into the
Cheering crowd.

The pitcher, shameless,
Raises mitt,
To stoke his own
Side's anger.

With air-borne beer
And plastic cups,
His crowd rains down
Its ire.

The umpire, meek,
Submits to them,
Allows a flag
To flutter,

Though not a one
Has seen an error.
Yet, he judges:
"Foul!"

The pitcher gloats.
And spits. And jigs.
With roaring
Adulation,

The crowd exacts
A strange revenge
Upon the
Winning team.

The winners watch,

In disbelief.
His strategy
Is working:

"Although the facts
betray our acts,
Let's lose--
And say we won."

Frat Boy Intro

7/28/21

I first saw the connection to fraternities in a tweet on July 27, 2021, calling Governor Ron DeSantis of Florida "CEO of The Delta House." This is my extrapolation on the theme.

As many of you know, I live in Florida. I have found little more infuriating than the positions the State has taken on the pandemic and how to handle it.

The latest surge in the Delta variant--which has now placed my own county at the forefront of affected areas in the US--has been met with stubborn assertions, that there will be no mask mandate, no masks in school, no local ordinances overriding the State's own laissez-faire rules, and no order lasting longer than 7 days at a time.

Local officials are powerless to combat the variant with stricter rules. And social-climbing Republican officials seize at the chance, to defy the CDC or other federal bodies, even their most common-sense recommendation of masking in schools, to protect our vulnerable and unvaccinated children. DeSantis got into trouble last week for referring to this practice as "muzzling" children.

"Freedom" is the clarion call of these advocates of inaction, and "individual responsibility" is their mantra.

Having gone to a school with a big Greek (sorority and fraternity) presence in the 1980's, I am vaguely aware of some of the excesses of frat boys. They drank too much. They did crazy things. They defied authority, just to show they could. They paraded their school pride, and then had their privileges taken away, when a particularly egregious hazing or a date rape showed up in the headlines. They were the cute guys, the ones with charisma, the ones with money and a girl on each arm. And yet, they didn't seem to give a damn for anyone outside of their club.

This is, of course, a negative portrayal of an obnoxious few--I am painting with a very broad brush.

But the way politicians are acting at this moment reminds me of that frat boy swagger: so lauded and extolled on one side, and so widely mocked, on the other.

Let us only hope that the officials tasked with our COVID response rise from their hangovers, wake up, and smell the coffee. Before it's too late.

Frat Boy

The opposite of common sense:
The vain erection of a fence.
The sworn protection of our rights,
The guarding of them, day and night:
Beside the point. Protect our lives.

The choice to be more free, than well,
Abhorring Regulation's Hell.
Forbidding simple blanket rules,
You take away our greatest tools,
And local leaders look like fools.

And We, The People? We believe.
In choosing for ourselves. Deceive
Us. Say we're better off this way,
That mandates have no part to play,

That there will be no Hell to pay.

Some watch one channel, get the shot.
Some watch another. They do not.
Some --worried shots are yet unproved,
And waiting, till their fears are soothed--
Run over, 'cause they failed to move.

This fight against the Nanny State--
What good is it? When you conflate
The value of The Constitution
With our weaker constitutions'
Health, you merely wreak confusion.

The opposite of common sense.
A macho, doctrinaire defense
Of rights, which simply have no bearing
On the question: Are we sharing
Germs, which kill each other off?
How can you turn away, and scoff?
And scurry off, a silent mouse?

So reigns the King of Delta House.

Flies Intro

8/5/2021

I came up with this idea while thinking about the news of the week.
- Capitol police, testifying about a mob, who voted the same way some of them did. A mob, who attacked the Capitol Police, even as they carried Blue Lives Matter flags. And while the Capitol Police testified about their harrowing, near-death experiences, prominent politicians mocked them and denied their version of reality, right outside the same building.

- Olympic athletes bowing out of the games, out of concern for their own mental health. Out of weariness, of the peering, intrusive eye of the media. Of the buzzing gadfly, that harasses every public figure, no matter their age or inner frailty.

- School districts, waging civil war amongst themselves, battling on camera, over the right to mask up our kids, or not. Insulting one another, draping themselves in the Constitution and the flag.

Whichever side of the debate they represent.

It seems that no matter what you do in this modern world, you will be attacked for it. And in a public, demeaning, callous way. And you are supposed to just take it.

When I first entered the legal profession, there were worries that people thought lawyers lacked civility.

Now, it seems like everyone does.

I hope, one day, we will approach our differences with more care and compassion.

Flies

Red neck cop
Chews tobacco, spits it out,
And shines his bumper sticker
With his shirtsleeve:
Blue Lives Matter.

Powerful, petite,
Black legs, pumping, locomotive
Twists and lands,
Each hair in place:
Shows up, for her country.

Harried mom
Ushers children to the car,
Backpacked, masked,
First day of school:

Brave, amidst an outbreak.

With our microscope, we see
The wrinkles and the fault-lines,
The errors people make,
Though they have done
Their very best.

Socrates, a gadfly,
Nimbly criticized decisions,
To hone a nobler character,
Or punish, when deserved.

But now, the swarm of flies is legion,
Clustered on each living corpse,
Attacking walking wounded,
Athletes, mothers-- anyone,

Who holds their head
Above the fray,
Protecting self,
Or family, country,

Daring, in their humble way,
To simply tell the truth.

Returning Boots Intro

9/1/2021

I wrote this poem after listening to a recent interview on *MSNBC Morning Joe* with two veterans, about their reactions to the recent pull-out from Afghanistan, completed on August 31, 2021. One veteran was the head of Team Rubicon, and the other was teaching a class on 9/11 to college students.

Some of the comments of the two veterans of the Afghan and Iraqi wars, are paraphrased in this poem.
- *Young adults in this country need to be **taught** about Nine-Eleven.* September 11, 2001, was when terrorists hit the World Trade Center buildings, in New York City, causing both towers to collapse. They also hit the Pentagon in Washington DC and tried to hit the US Capitol Building in Washington DC, all three attacks more or less simultaneous, with planes as weapons. Young people

need to be taught the importance of Nine-Eleven and what actually happened, because, unlike many of their elders, they have no memory of the event.

- *As veterans, they are still processing and trying to figure out how to think about the pull-out.* They are certainly not the only ones in this country with feelings of ambivalence.

- *The pullout hits military veterans differently than it does civilians.* That it hits them in a visceral way. Many of them have known or in some way been aided by Afghans who very well may not make it out. Also, many years of their lives have been devoted to this endeavor, and their identities are wrapped up in it. Any indication that they have wasted their time is a heavy blow.

- *America does not deserve its military, "so loyal, so good, so brave."* Blood, sweat and tears have protected this country (the US) during the past twenty years and well beyond, but many veterans feel unseen and unrecognized despite their valiant effort.

I guess this poem is my own attempt to process the event. I am not a veteran, nor do I have any veterans of this war in my immediate family. This was another point of the discussion, that the Afghan war was fought by people many of us never met. As for me, the idea of the Taliban or any iteration of that group taking over again, sends shivers down my spine. I worry for the Afghan women. All I can think is, what is former First Lady Laura Bush thinking now? I remember her impassioned plea in the early 2000's, to save those oppressed women from their terrible fate.

I do not know how the pullout could have been done better. Or whether it would have been better, had we stayed. Only time will tell.

Returning Boots

Nine babies born, aboard a plane,
Chock-full of refugees.
Americans and Afghans.
Full-length burqas. Barren knees.

For twenty years, the babies born
Have known no Nine-Eleven.
It's over. So, they must be taught
Those martyrs' stab at Heaven.

And here, at home, nigh on two weeks,
It's been a veteran's Hell.
The promises they must have made
Have all gone down the well.

POLEMICS: POLITICAL POEMS & PROSE

What was it for? What good was done?
Such noble sacrifice...
While we at cozy TVs sat,
The Gold Stars paid the price.

Now, thirteen more--and countless Afghans--
Fertilize the chaos.
A bombing taunts our weak retreat,
With tail between our legs.

While veterans are "processing,"
Our leaders misbehave,
And run to shelter cul-de-sacs,
As turbaned heads invade.

Here's your reward, Afghanistan,
For planning Nine-Eleven:
A martyrdom, for all your dead,
And virgins, ninety-seven.

Our land no longer gives a hoot.
Take back your dust and caves.
We don't deserve returning boots:
So loyal,
So good,
So brave.

Regrets Intro

11/22/21

    This poem came to me while driving into a very reddish sunset. At first, I thought it was a short story, some kind of science fiction about the end of the world. But the repetition and rhyme were too insistent. Hope you enjoy this story-poem and take a lesson or two from it.

Regrets

The astronomer told
The late-born son,
The fruit of his loins,
His precious one,
"In seventy years,
The sun will die.
And sooner, so will I."

"I'll never survive
The late-born sun,"
The late-born son
Replied, to one
With grizzled beard
And blinded eye.
"In fact, I'm sure, I'll die."

With grinning lips
And twinkling eye,
The son, he gave
This glib reply,
So bright with glee,
To think that he
Could ever be so old.

The grizzled gent,
He slowly bent
And crossed himself,
Chastised the elf:
"No one should wish that
On himself!
No one should be so bold!"

"I'll never survive
The late-born sun,"
The late-born son replied.
"Why should I bother
To try? Not one
Will suffer, if I've
Nothing done,
Least of all me.
My progeny?
I leave no booty to them."

"But all will die!
Humanity!
Not a soul be saved--
Insanity!
And an early grave
Is the price you'd pay,
To avoid your duty to them?"

"I'll never survive
The late-born sun,"
The late-born son
Repeated.
"When the ball is red
On horizon's edge,
And is falling, falling
Off that ledge,
And it's fiery hot
And it glows and glows,
And the sky above
Is a deep, red rose,
And the sheepskin clouds
Warm the sherpa's nose,
As he scales the frigid blue--
I'll be gone,
When the sun,
At last, it sets.
No son of yours
Shall have regrets.
And none, then, shall resemble you."

"Alas," said the sage. "None do."

The Lawman Intro

1/7/2022

    This is a poem about loyalists, resisting the grind of the wheels of justice, in defense of their favorite.

The Lawman

"Just politics,"
The lawman said
As he stared at the TV.
"They're trying to ruin
His reputation.
With the facts, they're free.

"They're trying to find
A smoking gun.
His gun ain't never smoked!
They'll never find
A thing on him."
The scoffing lawman spoke.

The witnesses,
The paper stacks,

The emails and the texts...
"They don't 'mount to
A hill of beans!"
The lawman screams. "What's next?!"

The lesser aides,
The perp parades,
The men behind closed doors:
"It's just for show!
What do they know?
To prove it, they need more."

The gutless guilty
Huddle, and
Subpoenas, they defy.
Referrals go
To Justice,
But "It's just a pack of lies!

"Why should they
Make appearances?
Subpoenas have no power!
So what, if they
Are in contempt?
Or in a prison's bower?

"These men are
Heroes, to defy
An all-intrusive State!
I bet they'd
Summon Santa,
If his reindeer showed up late!"

And yet, each day
Another trickle

Leaks out to the Press.
"What difference
Does that make?
The news is fake!" the lawman says.

"We don't need
No Commission!
It's a waste of tax and time!
We should be
Making laws,
Not raking over ancient crimes!"

At last, it
Hits the papers
And explodes across the page:
The smoking gun!
He is the one,
The butt of blame and rage.

The lawman
And compatriots
Sit threesome in a row.
One holds his eyes.
One holds his ears.
And one, his lips won't show.

"You never will
Convince me!"
Shouts the lawman. "It's a draw!
For I reject
Your premise:
I reject The Rule of Law."

Déjà vu Intro

1/21/2022

    I wrote this poem after listening to an interchange between Joe Scarborough of *Morning Joe on MSNBC* and Jon Meacham, the historian, on January 31, 2022. They were talking about the notion of a "stolen" election.

    They reminded me about the election in 2000, and how raw the wound felt to those of us in Florida who voted for Al Gore, the Democrat. And how it remained tender, long after the election.

    For those of you who don't remember, in Florida, there was only a very small sliver of votes--only five hundred or so--between the candidates. So, a recount was ordered. But before the recount could be completed, the appellate case against the decision to hold a recount made its way up to the Supreme Court of the United States. Very quickly, the Supreme Court halted the recount. In between these events, the progress of the recount was nightly news, and the whole nation wondered what would happen next.

What happened next will seem astounding in our day and age. Al Gore got up and gave a profoundly patriotic concession speech. He stepped aside, so the Republican candidate, George Bush, could transition into office peacefully and so the nation could heal.

He could have launched an insurrection, I suppose, or incessantly beat his drum about how the election was stolen from him, or he could have defied the Constitutional system of how electors are chosen, by trying to maneuver around the count or control it somehow.

But he didn't.

So, my question is this: Although it may seem, technically, as if we have been here before (hence the title, *Deja Vu*) have we really? In 2000, the losing candidate landed on the side of finality and union. Hard to say that, about 2020.

Déjà vu

How we shuddered, how we shook
Our heads, dismayed: Five hundred votes.
Hanging chads. Repeated countings.
Challenging results in court.

And so it went. For many weeks,
We trained the spotlight on our state.
The nation stretched on tenterhooks,
To learn its outcome, seal its fate.

We called it "Stolen!" when we heard
The verdict from the highest court.
We cried, to watch the Secretary
Certify the half-done count.

But then, a man, a great, great man,

Acknowledged that the loss was his,
And rallied us to love our
Constitution, marvel, that it is.

For even when the chips are down,
And we have lost our every cent,
Yes, even then, we must accept
Elections make a president.

And though, up top, the lure of power
Is overwhelming, absolute,
We poll the masses every four years,
Growing only from the root.

Again, the chant of "Stolen! Stolen!"
Rings upon our eager ears.
And anger mounts, and vicious lies
Divide the sides, inflate our fears.

How perfect, for pretenders
Who'd extend their shortened stay!
Where's that man who stands, admits?
We need finality, today.

False Equivalencies Intro

2/11/2022

    In this poem, I try to point out how we often talk about issues as if there were only one side to them. This is not so much a left vs. right argument, as it is a plea for nuance in our thinking and for genuine truth-seeking.

    The idea came from a quote I heard by George Packer, on the withdrawal from Afghanistan. He used the delicious phrases, "the precious attention of the US government" and the "tender mercies of the Taliban." It was a prime example of how the bumbling of a superpower is not equal, in its measure of evil, to the cruelty of tyrants.

    The Taliban, of course, is the group that took power in Afghanistan when the US left, just as they had earlier held the country, before we arrived on the scene. In their last iteration, they were well known for public executions and mistreatment of women. May they, in the future, exceed our dim expectations.

The reference to the shining city on a hill is from the closing of Ronald Reagan's 1988 State of the Union Address and apparently his 1989 farewell address as well. He refers to a Puritan speech by a pastor named Winthrop who got his reference from the Bible,

> Ye are the light of the world. A city that is set on a(n) hill cannot be hid.
> Matthew 5:14 King James Version

For a more recent and much more thorough discussion of a book about the relevance of the city on a hill speech to today's America, read The Atlantic's story, *Is America Still A Shining City on a Hill?* by David Frum, from January 2021.

False Equivalencies

The sluggish machinations of the government.
The swift and tender mercies of the Taliban.

The quiet indignation of the oppressed hurt.
The pouting cries for fairness from the wealthy man.

The back-broken farmer digging up the soil.
The preppie pushing buttons for a market trade.

The middle-aged gun-nut rising to a boil.
The tiny child who pulls a trigger in his play.

The rugged blue policeman toiling to keep peace.
The one who keeps a knee upon the black man's neck.

The hippies at the protest chanting "Let us be!"
The traitors, still not swinging from their hairy necks.

The man who knows the inside of a prison cell.
The man who should but never stains his bespoke clothes.

The man who wears a mask to ward off being ill.
The man who masks to steal and garner others' votes.

The words repeated, researched and informed by fact.
The words, we aim like weapons, with intent to kill.

This darkest night of falsehood will remain intact
Till Truth be-lights our shining city on a hill.

Grateful Intro

3/24/2022

As the weeks drag on, my disappointment in our government's--and frankly the West's--response to the Ukraine situation grows, resulting in this bitter poem. It is told from the point of view of a leader whose country is under attack, and is addressed to his allies. One can well imagine Zelenskyy feeling this way, although these are not his words. Sorry to use such a tired idiom at the end, but--as they say--when the shoe fits!

On a lighter note, I highly recommend the Ukrainian TV show now on Netflix with subtitles, *Servant of the People*. It's a lighthearted show, made before Zelenskyy was elected, that probes the ideals of Western Democracy in the face of corruption and nepotism.

Ukrainian President Volodymyr Zelenskyy (who started his career as a comedian) stars, ironically, as a history teacher turned Ukrainian President. In addition to being very funny, he has so many unintentionally prophetic lines, which, in light of current events, make you cringe. You also have a chance to see how beautiful Kiev was, before all this happened.

Grateful

You ask, am I grateful
For kindly outpourings
Of sympathy, comments
And follows and likes?
You ask, am I grateful
For armaments coming
And drones, anti-aircraft,
Munitions, to fight?

You ask, am I grateful
For sanctions that bankrupt,
And weaken the currency,
De-fund the foe?
You ask, am I grateful
For neighbors nearby,
With their NATO-soft lives,

ANDREA W LEDEW

Taking refugees home?

You ask, am I grateful
For standing ovations,
For yet-tougher sanctions
When lesser ones fail?
You ask, am I grateful
Reporters reporting
In dangerous quarters
Keep telling the tale?

You ask, am I grateful
For businesses leaving,
When mothers are grieving
Their children today?
You ask, am I grateful
They're lending a hand,
When they don't understand
Bodies, thrown in mass graves?

You ask, am I grateful
For all the donations,
For money to burn
In this three-alarm fire?
You ask, am I grateful
For help, in ground warfare,
When bombs keep on dropping
From higher and higher?

My friends, I *am* grateful.
The West is amazing.
Can't wait to join NATO--
When NATO lets me.
It's hard to be grateful,
When down on your knees.

With buddies like you,
I don't need
Enemies.

Litmus Test Intro

5/04/22

This week's headline news included a leak of a non-final draft decision by Supreme Court Justice Samuel Alito. It dealt with the question of whether to overturn the 50-year-old decision **Roe v Wade**, which protects a pregnant woman's right to choose whether or not to have a child, by means of terminating her early pregnancy, through legalized abortion.

The prematurely leaked draft--much like the unexpected pregnancies it affects-- surprised many. It was a forceful vote to completely overturn the decision. The Supreme Court has, in recent years, been more incremental in its approach, chipping away at the protections of **Roe**, bit by bit. The idea that this might finally be the case that does away with **Roe**, once and for all, has many in the press and public up at arms, while others cheer.

I found it interesting to hear a commentator observe that since the 1980's, abortion has been exploited as a wedge issue with ever more success.

Before 1980, positions on abortion crossed party lines. Now, it is essentially used as a litmus test for all those who would run for office on a Republican ticket. Unless you can prove you are anti-abortion, do not even bother to apply.

For those who do not recall high school chemistry class (and I, for one, had to look it up to refresh my memory), a litmus test is a common test of acid or base pH values in an aqueous liquid. There are blue strips and red strips, and each turns the opposite color when dipped into a solution which is acidic or base. Blue turns red when dipped in an acid (<7.0 pH) Red turns blue when dipped in a base (or alkaline) liquid (>7.0 pH).

In foods, for example, meat and sodas are more acidic and vegetables more base. Hydrochloric acid and bleach are more acidic and baser still, respectively, than anything we could safely take into our own, slightly alkaline bodies. Neutral liquids, such as water, provide a purple result in either type of strip.

The test is quite old. It was apparently originally developed using a distillation of lichens from the Netherlands, by a Spanish physician named Arnaldus de Villa in 1300 AD. The word litmus comes from a Norse word meaning "dye" or "color."

The fact that Democrats identify with the color blue and Republicans with the color red make the metaphor that much easier to apply. I also find it funny that despite the color alignments, Republicans (red) are always the ones trying to rally their base (blue.)

So, instead of arguing about who is right on this controversial question, why don't we instead ask ourselves whether it is wise to divide ourselves from our fellow citizens, Democrat vs. Republican, young vs. old, woman vs. man, on a perplexing question as old as Time.

Litmus Test

Plop a drop upon a blotter.
Watch the color morph and turn.
One result will chart your leanings,
Your belonging, Us or Them.

Test with strips of red and blue,
Distilled within a Middle Age,
Work of a Spanish physician, before
The Inquisition was the rage.

A test of acid Red or basic
Blue or neutral Purple hue
Divides us into categories:
Us and Them, not Me and You.

And how we think upon a subject,

Where we lie, which side of seven,
Betrays us, in our brother's eye,
As of the Devil, or of Heaven.

Which are you? More red? More blue?
Would we reject all foodstuffs thus,
And throw away our meats and veg,
Each different, so, despised by us?

And now, one question parts a nation--
Moses, and the Red-Blue Sea--
Till Pharaoh comes, with all his men.
T'will be the end of You and Me.

Scores Intro

5/25/22

This poem derives its title and somewhat embellished content from President Joe Biden's speech, responding to the shooting at an elementary school in Uvalde, Texas, on May 24, 2022.

Nineteen children were killed, and two adults.

Just a week before, another mass shooting, inspired by racial hatred and documented with a manifesto online, took place in a grocery store in Buffalo, NY. Most of the victims were elderly and black.

Children inspire a special kind of grief, as evidenced by the 24-7 news coverage of this latest incident. But we must remember that all lives are equally precious.

During his speech, Biden expressed compassion for the victims' families. He asked "Why?" and expressed the same embarrassed befuddlement we all feel, when we take note of the fact that this seems to happen more often here, in the US, than anywhere else.

Statistically speaking, it should not be so. Morally speaking, it should not be so.

Often, in his speeches, Biden refers to grief. He has a certain familiarity with it, having lost both a spouse and children over time.

In this speech, he used the somewhat antiquated term "scores." He was referring to the number of children lost to school mass shootings over time (not to mention those lost in other, more mundane incidents of gun violence. If the death of a child can ever be described as "mundane.") A score refers to a group of twenty.

When we hear "score," we recall the famous Gettysburg Address by another president, Abraham Lincoln. Lincoln was speaking in a time of bloody Civil War. In that speech, which begins "Four-score and seven years ago..." Lincoln asked Americans to resolve "that these dead shall not have died in vain..."

In his speech, Biden may have been even more plainspoken than honest Abe. But let us hope that his simple words will also inspire great change.

The nation grieves for the families of the recent victims and, I hope, for the families of all who have fallen to gun violence in years past. I am sorry if it seems "too soon." But as Biden pointed out, when does it ever seem like a good time to speak a terrible truth?

Scores

I know your pain.
I feel your pain.
With grief, I'm well-acquainted.
I've lived. Which means,
My friends have died.
My wife. And yes, my children.

They point at me.
I speak too soon,
The wound still raw and bleeding.
What, should I wait
Till you stop crying?
Then, express compassion?

What makes us hate?
What makes the young

Pull out a gun and shoot it?
T'would be no less
A tragedy,
If we but understood it.

"Fourscore and seven
Kids ago..."
(If only it were so few)
Would make a speech
More memorable
Than what I say to you.

As President,
I'm powerless.
Each life a brittle thread.
But give a gun
To anyone
And boom! A child is dead.

I can't explain it,
Can't prevent it,
Over and over again,
With all the shock
And horror of
A looping World War film.

Ten years ago,
Another school.
Another parent, weeping.
Nine hundred shootings
In between:
Why have we all been sleeping?

A child, a shopper:
Does it matter

ANDREA W LEDEW

Whom the bullet fells?
No reason could be
Good enough
To put you through this hell.

No manifesto,
Scrawled in pencil.
No desire for fame.
He turned a gun
Upon his own.
Yet we are all to blame.

I'm sick and tired
Of Thoughts and Prayers,
Disputing shades of gray.
I know your pain.
I've lost a child.
But Jesus,
Not this way.

Dystopia Today Intro

6/25/22

This poem comes on the heels of the Supreme Court *Dobbs* decision, overturning *Roe vs. Wade*. *Roe* has stood for fifty years for the right of a woman to make unilateral decisions about her own body, even when she is pregnant, at least early on in the pregnancy.

I have not read the new case yet, but the news media are proclaiming the death of *Roe*. This decision vindicates the movement which, for twenty years or more, has made it its mission to overturn the case. One of their ingenious methods was to produce legions of lawyers and judges and officials who, in good conscience, could argue and legislate against it.

I did not actually believe this could happen in my lifetime. I went to law school at a time when law and morality/religion were seen as separate. It is true that one protected and was informed by the other. But law was not driven by morality, especially not by the morality of a specific niche group. And especially not when that morality conflicted with the interests of others.

Cognitive dissonance is the sense that something is off, or not quite right, because you are holding two opposing thoughts in your head at the same time. This problem occurs frequently in law, and we tolerate it, as long as individual rights are protected.

For example, we all hate death, especially preventable death. We abhor murder, the deliberate taking of the life of another. So can it ever be right or moral to forsake the life of one, for the life of another? Perhaps not. But it can under certain circumstances be legal. *Roe* was until recently one such instance.

Similarly, things that seem patently wrong are allowed by law: Hate groups can march. A certain amount of behavior that might be distasteful to some of us is tolerated, to protect the individual rights of all.

During the January 6th Hearings currently on TV, you hear a lot of talk about "The Oath," not to be confused with the Oathkeepers, a far right hate group. The oath requires the Constitution, *rather than a single man*, to be the focus of loyalty for officers of the court and government officials.

I think this holds true for ideas as well. Whether it be religious or political or in some other realm, when *loyalty to an idea is so great that it overwhelms ones loyalty to the Constitution* of our great country, bad things can happen. We cannot afford to allow people driven by ideology to determine the meaning of the Constitution.

Of course, those who rejoice in yesterday's decision will say that the Court has always been driven by ideology. They will argue that, in fact, it was ideology that gave birth to *Roe*, so to speak. One might question whether it is even possible for a human being to strip all belief from his or her decision-making process. But belief is a strange and dangerous thing, in that it tends to have both beneficiaries and victims.

Whichever way you look at it, this decision is an important milestone. Many believe *Roe* to be the seminal decision, so to speak, allowing women to participate in the workforce, in business, and in their personal lives, as powerful, independent and, dare I say, *equal* beings to men.

With this new *Dobbs* decision in place, will women of child-bearing age once again be slaves to their own fertility? Time will tell. I hope we have a long way to go before we reach the kind of dystopia described in the fiction of Margaret Atwood's *The Handmaid's Tale*. But as people like to say in the legal profession, it's a slippery slope.

Sorry for the darkness. I do not create it. I merely reflect what I see.

Dystopia Today

What's right is wrong.
What's wrong is right.
And all is upside down.
We're entering Dystopia,
The province of the clown.

What's white is black.
What's black is white.
Lies nothing in between?
We're entering Dystopia,
The province of the mean.

And everyone is equal here
Though some have lesser rights.

They want to make us better,
Sweeter, spoil us for the fight.

For Progress can but go so far
Upon its escapade,
Before it shifts into reverse,
And speeds in retrograde.

What's new is old. What's old is new.
Intent shall chart the course,
And soon we'll be awash in poxes,
Plodding, on a horse,

As if it never happened:
Fifty years, approaching Fair.
Now get ye to your kitchens!
You will find small comfort there.

A country grasping God, and trampling
Subjects on the way.
You're welcome to Dystopia.
Dystopia, today.

Remarkably Indecent Intro

6/29/2022

In this poem, I string together various quotes from the course of the day yesterday, after Cassidy Hutchinson gave her testimony at the January 6th Hearings. The first two lines were stolen from the very serious lawyer and MSNBC commentator, Chuck Rosenberg, and were said, almost word for word, in direct reaction to the testimony.

The focus of the day's testimony seemed to be character-- that of President Trump, his Chief of Staff Mark Meadows, and various other people in the West Wing, such as the assistant Chief of Staff and Trump's driver, and even the witness herself. But the *real question* for the country is*: what is the character of the electorate?* That is what will determine our future.

Hope you enjoy this barbed reaction to the day's shocking revelations. "Mags," by the way, means magnetometers, or metal detector machines, used to screen the crowd for weapons. "The Beast" is a nickname for the

President's limousine. Ms. Hutchinson mistakenly called the SUV, that he was actually riding in on January 6, "The Beast."

Remarkably Indecent

Remarkably indecent, vile,
And yes, uncivil man,
Who hurls a burger at the wall
And lurches, in a van,
To reach the steering wheel,
Attack a man, who'd step into
The line of fire to keep him safe.
To keep him safe, from You.

But You, You are his people.
You would never hurt a fly--
Upon his person--with your weapons,
Armed, as is your right.
Though, rather strange—You'd fight against

The birds? You'd climb a tree?
"Take down the mags," your idol says.
"They're not here, to hurt ME."

What knowledge lurks within that brain,
Which plays the winsome fool?
A genius--for manipulating.
Callous, crass and cruel.
Whose like we've never seen before,
In many, many a moon.
Who'd say, it's right to hang his Vice.
Or hurl him 'cross a room.

What's that you say? He never lost?
You say, he'll run again?
This time, You'll make damn sure that he's
Not kept from getting in
The White House, his anointed home,
By petty votes. For shame!
You think you can control this Beast?
Create a statesman, tame?

You'd sooner lasso you a windstorm.
Yet, You play his game.
Barometer is off the charts:
A moral hurricane.

Free Speech Intro

9/4/2022

    This poem started out as an anthem for writers. So many of us, who have this incomprehensible urge to share our thoughts, are nonetheless burdened with a quiet, introverted nature, which abhors all grandstanding. This poem was originally meant to urge writers to be more bold in sharing and promoting their work. One writer in particular, of course. Me.

    But as I wrote, I came across the rather poorly hidden sarcasm in the poem. It could just as easily be read as a condemnation of someone, who is a little too free with his or her ideas, to the detriment of those who listen. Especially since I wrote it, shortly after watching two political documentaries on the events leading up to January 6, 2021: *Unprecedented* and *Assault on Democracy*.

    What particularly struck me about the first documentary was the comment Ivanka Trump made about her father, praising him for his honesty and forthrightness. As a person from the opposite camp, I laughed out loud at this remark.

But then I realized that, whether demonstrably, factually true or not, *Trump's comments do register as true,* to a certain audience. That is, they perceive Trump's words as being an accurate description of reality, consistent with their experience and belief.

I think in general, people who seem candid, who appear to lay their cards on the table, seem more trustworthy and believable, than those who hold their cards close to their chest. Only with experience do we learn to recognize, that dastardly but most congenial salesman, whose friendly, sincere purpose is to swindle us out of all that we possess.

Perhaps, rather than as an ode to Free Speech, this poem should be read as a warning. Perhaps we should be more circumspect in what we say. Because, as we so often hear said, words have consequences.

Yet another way to view --or hear--this poem is as a call to all of us, to be just as loud in our refutations, as the loudest voice in the room is, spouting his or her lies. The irony of free speech is, that it is not the monopoly of the right (nor the Right.) *The only way to ensure that the wrong do not prevail is for the right to step up and speak.* And drown them out, with even more compelling, but equally free, speech.

Free Speech

Force your voice upon the world.
Say your piece out loud.
Ring your bell at highest knell.
Of yourself, be proud.

Bare your candle to the wind.
Fill your bushel full.
Weep your tears down to your chin.
Trade your bear for bull.

Walk with swagger in your stride.
Let the public stare.
Let them criticize, deride.
Though your bum be bare,

Make apologies to none.

Tell them what you see.
Lure them with your Piper's song.
No Speech attracts, like Free.

The Swindler Intro

10/19/2022

    My daughter has gone to work as an intern in a great estate garden in Southeastern England. I hear from her from time to time, and most recently she sent me a video of a rip-roaring old sea shanty. It was sung and performed in a barn by one of her co-workers, with his audience joining in, for the chorus.

    Nowadays, with all the talk of swindles and political misdeeds in the news, I felt inspired to create a kind of sea shanty of my own, about a swindler getting her come-uppance. I have conformed the language and dress to what I imagine they might have used in earlier, seafaring days.

    I'd love to hear it performed in the same manner as my daughter's coworker did his, with nothing but clapping and a singalong at the chorus, as accompaniment. I admit, that it may not have quite met the high standards of bawdiness and humor one expects from a sea shanty. It certainly doesn't have much to do with the sea. The tune that plays in my head when I read it is *The Marvelous Toy,* by Peter Paul and Mary. Think of your favorite swindler, as you read or sing along!

For you English majors and grammarians, I have left out much of punctuation to enhance the continuous nature of these songs. They are best performed going from verse to verse, almost without a breath. Forgive my well-intentioned lapses!

The Swindler

Lucy Tulip Battersbea
Was a favorite of the knaves
And no old codgers found it odd,
When she danced upon their graves.

She had an inclination
To found a fashion house,
Her fashion sense, small recompense
For the men she would espouse
To fund her schemes. A twinkle
In her artful, winsome eye
Would land, hook, line and sinker,
The prey that she espied.

And were they once to wriggle,
To escape her pretty grasp,

She would jerk the line, knowing all the time,
That she only need to ask
For she had a set of dimples,
And a pouty mouth to boot,
And a figure rounded and compounded,
Fine, for stealing loot.

And she listened like an innocent,
Like putty in their hands
But when after all, they checked their wallets--
Gone! Or I'll be damned!
Oh, Lucy Tulip Battersbea
Was a maid not to be trusted.
Man after man watched her flim and flam
And soon those men were busted.

But along came Bob O'Brien,
In his waistcoat and his hat,
And Lucy's eyes could spy his silver
Watch, and that was that
And she hooked her arm round his hoary elbow,
Fumbling for his coins,
But he saw her mischief, shook his head,
And ignored his stirring loins.

And he asked her "Miss? What fraud is this?
What drivel and what blather?
You'd sooner love a knave than me!
Why flirt with a cadaver?"
"Oh, I'd love to fund a fashion house,"
Cooed Lucy to her prey.
"I'm short on cash but thought I'd ask.
You're looking sharp, today!"

"I've heard about you, pretty thing,"

ANDREA W LEDEW

The magnate tipped his hat,
"Not a single farthing shall you have."
He vowed. His fingers snapped
And behind him came the constable
And they took her off in irons.
And Darling Lucy rued the day
She swindled Bob O'Brien.

Who Owns My Vote? Intro

11/08/2022

 I came up with this poem on Election Day 2022, as the Midterm Elections in the US began to blanket the morning news. I accompanied it with a photo of me in my *Bitter Southerner* t-shirt, urging everyone to cast their vote.
 One odd thing about this election is the number of people who are running, who, even so, seem to question the very system that allows them to gain office.
 The idea of overturning the 2020 election, as some seem eager to do, is problematic to me for one simple reason. I can think of no one who holds the power to take a vote away from a person, once they have cast it. Does each voter somehow relinquish ownership of their own vote with the very act of voting, so that the outcome is now subject to manipulation or second-guessing? I think not.

I think a redo would require the consent of all the voters, especially all those who voted for the eventual certified outcome. The noise about questioning the 2020 election, at its heart, relies on the assumption, that a vote, once cast, belongs to whoever is in power, to do with as they see fit.

This poem is an attempt to answer the question once and for all. Who does a vote belong to?

Be sure to use yours.

Who Owns My Vote?

Who owns my vote?
I held it last
Two years ago:
A blotted sheet
Of legal size,
Though even legal
Minds now use the letter.

Who owns my vote?
Who gets to draw
The hem and haw
Of darkened bubbles?
Who insists
I vote for this--

Or that--dull proposition?

Who owns my vote?
Conspiracies
May darken seas
And roil the waves;
Misinformation,
Fog the issues,
Cause confusion,
Plant despair.

Who owns my vote?
Shrill cries abound:
Apocalypse!
Democracy
Is dying,
Like a baby
In an alleyway,
Neglected.

Who owns my vote?
What power decides
Which choice resides
Within my pen?
Who dictates to me,
Where or when
I exercise
This fragile right?

Who owns my vote?
Who gets me up
And gets me dressed
And guides my feet--
Or wheels--to this
Vast church

Gymnasium
Or mason's lodge?

Who owns my vote?
Who makes me wait
In lines, when I
Should be at work
or watching kids
Or sleeping?
Who insists
I wait my turn?

Who owns my vote?
What man can change it,
Once it's cast?
Who, rearranging
Districts,
Gerrymandering,
Can make
My ballot moot?

Who owns my vote?
Am I beholden
To some golden boy,
Some group?
Has all
The secrecy,
Protecting me,
Left every ballot?

Who owns my vote?
Have wives not cast
Their votes to cancel
Out their man's,
When their self-interest

So demanded,
Needing
No consent?

Who owns my vote,
I ask of you.
Is this a hazing
I go through,
To show
That I belong,
like you?
Or independent thought?

Who owns my vote?
What power can change it,
After due
Consideration?
Slap me, right
Upside my head,
And on a whim,
Correct me?

No man can do this.
Only I.
I make the choice--
Or fail -- to do
What every citizen
Should do--
Decide--
Three hundred
Million strong--
And none corrupt us,
String along
Our harmonies—
We sing one song.

Who owns my vote?
I do.

The End Intro

3/21/23

If you watched with horror, as banks crumbled (or crumpled?) this week, this poem's for you! From what I have read about SVG Bank, the Original Gangster of this present bank run, it was heavily concentrated in business from one sector: Tech.

And I thought morality plays were no longer in fashion.

Let us hope, that we have already seen the Worst. And yet prepare, as if the Worst is yet to come.

The End

The age of the Specialist is at an end.
Expertise leads to nothing but trouble.
Concentrating your resources means, you can't fend
Off a panic, if panic redoubles.

Perhaps it's just happenstance, leading your steps
To a place where the Everyman reigns,
Where the Jack of All Trades and the Generalist
Can evade all the Specialist's pains.

All your eggs in one basket? I'd recommend two,
Maybe three, maybe four at the least.
We now know that one industry barely said "Boo!"
And a mouse slayed the King of the Beasts.

I suppose, for a runner, a bank run is fun,

ANDREA W LEDEW

As he chases his cash down the drain,
But if friends tell their friends, well, the fun never ends,
Breaking links, in an orderly chain.

You can open your eyes! Yes, the panic is over.
Collect up your stock market ticker.
Though the tape may dismay, you'll forget it, one day.
Maybe then, your demise will be quicker.

Ampersands Intro

6/25/2023

Most of you are probably familiar with the ampersand. The symbol looks like this: **&**

The symbol means "and."

It occurred to me, and perhaps you have had the same thought, that the inclusion movements throughout our history have been a *constant process of addition*: gradually adding more and more people to the register of those, whom we consider equals.

Of course, if you read the Constitution literally, you might believe that from the beginning, everyone has always been "created equal." But ask people of any race besides white, any gender besides male, any sexual preference besides hetero, and you will find those that tend to disagree.

I play, in this poem, with the rainbow imagery so prevalent this time of year. It is Pride Month, and many hang rainbow flags to indicate alignment with the cause. I explore how our motivations are sometimes performative, infused with the hope, that we will be perceived as nice, tolerant people.

Unfortunately, as the constant back and forth of our own Florida state politics has shown, progress in one direction--toward equality--is often followed by a period of regression, back toward the previous status quo. Religion, tradition, and deep-set beliefs stand in the way of what may seem like simple equality, to those who seek it.

I also point out, that the rainbow is a spectrum. This brings to mind the autism spectrum. The *Inclusion* that autistic individuals have had to fight for, and which still is an imperfect, partial thing, has also been stymied by the realities of life. Money, time, safety, independence or lack thereof, and the aging of those, whose natural role is to care for them.

In color theory, a spectrum includes opposites, contrasting colors—colors, that, when combined, form browns and blacks and grays. Even while decorating, few people include the entire spectrum in their palette. Even less so, in their social circle. Stirring the pot which contains all types of people means combining combustible, opposing forces.

I am not saying that being intolerant of difference is a good thing. I am only saying that intolerance exists. The existence of opposition was a fact when people sought to abolish slavery, and when they sought to have their civil rights recognized.

Each gain is hard won, and is pushed back upon, as soon as our backs are turned. And even if our idealism might lead us to believe that equality is achievable now, intolerance and pushback must be reckoned with.

Here in this poem, I mull over the seedy side of even the most well-meaning and purposeful movements toward greater inclusion. Movements such as the one that is heralded and celebrated during Pride Month. And I wish everyone better luck from now on, in convincing our flawed human race to do what's right.

Ampersands

This rainbow--jeweled spectrum--
With trembling bands of light,
Its sibling strands and ampersands
Contrast, combine, to night.

While cheery-colored opposites
Upon the color wheel
Would seem to strike a contrast,
When combined, these tones reveal

Our muddy thoughts and instincts,
For humanity hates change,
Admiring difference--at a distance.
Close, we re-arrange

The palette, cull, to suit our needs,

Traditional and bland.
We pick two colors, maybe three,
And toss the ampersand.

What use have we for everyone?
Too many spoils the clique.
Inclusion breeds confusion.
Stirring all will dull the mix.

This flag hangs proud upon my porch,
They walk by and they know.
But have I friends of every hue?
The answer, simply: No.

Our simpering claims of openness
Apply to what we know.
Yet throw some strangeness in the mix,
And watch our colors' glow

Devolve, to churning thunderclouds
And storms that howl and twist.
And watch our union disappear,
Less rainbow now, than mist.

Kangaroo Court (Honeypot) Intro

5/31/24

    This tongue-in-cheek poem, rather inappropriately, uses the familiar children's story of *Winnie the Poo*h by A.A. Milne to frame some recent current events. "Kangaroo Court" is an expression meaning a court with no authority. "Honeypot" or "honey trap" can mean a device used by spies, to lure in and trap their prey, in a compromising, blackmailable position, usually through a sexual encounter. This was penned during a week in which Trump's legal trouble with Stormy Daniels was much in the news.

Kangaroo Court (Honeypot)

What's that in your pocket?
Tiny little Roo,
Snuggling with Kanga,
Questioning poor Pooh.

Sweet interrogation.
Simple little facts.
Stories for a jury
Sitting in a box.

What will happen to me?

Have I misbehaved?
Will they see right through me?
Will I get away?

Rumbles in my tummy.
Hunger doesn't lie.
Let me ride balloon strings
Right up to the sky,

Close enough, to grab some
Honey on my paw.
Will the bees get angry?
Worser, will the law?

Eeyore's just a donkey,
Always seeing black.
Piglet is my bestie.
Always has my back.

Just 'cause they convict me
Doesn't mean I'll pay.
Heffalumps support me
Even when I stray.

Nobody can catch me.
I'm above the law.
Clinging to balloon strings.
Sticky, sticky paws.

I'm a bear and can't be
Something that I'm not.
If only I could get my head out
Of this honeypot.

Gray Galleons Intro

7/3/2024

    This poem talks about the upcoming 2024 Presidential race, with two men, each well in excess of seventy years old, facing off.

Gray Galleons

Our Lady Justice, thumb on the scale,
Licks the opposite index finger, pokes the air,
And tests the tropical wind of opinion.
Up the steps, overfamiliar and greedy,
Hot air rises, ruffling her hair.
Her blindfold slips a bit. No matter.
All will be well. No need to fear.

A ghost stands on a stage, agape.
Agape is our only hope:
The love of God for human beings,
Against His better judgment.
These two were loved and blessed and tossed
By the winds of time. Cruelty and kindness,
Dealt to them, in equal measure.
Refusing to be sunk, they licked their wounds,

Survived to sail, again.

Gray galleons, on a collision course,
Decrepit, stinking of decay,
Each would lead our legions to the future.
For it takes too long, it's too much trouble
To turn those ships around.
Once victory is achieved, what then?
Our captains point to one another.
With him, you'll ride to Armageddon.
Only I can save you.

And why should we believe a word?
As if the podium instills
In all who touch it, Truth,
So even now, your lies turn golden.
It's a Golden Age we live in. One
Where humans live forever.
A Neverland, full of crooks and pirates
Pillaging, unhindered,
And parentless boys who follow blindly,
Still believing in pixie dust.

The old have always been ridiculous.
With cracks and caverns, lacking youth and beauty,
They fall asleep on stage or in a courtroom,
Awaken, cranky, from their furtive dreams,
Hearing still, in their ears, the distant clanking
Of the ghosts who've gone before.
Unamused, they are the butt of everyone's jokes.

How briefly we luxuriated
In the calm of dull normality.
That's well over, now. Back to the docks.
Back to the battle with cannons and rams.

Back to the choking scent of gunpowder
And the deafening triumph of actions, over words.
Here shall we lay our final bets.

Businesses smile at the roiling markets,
Ready to fish out fleeing rats,
Hoping, even in the highest swells,
To land on their feet, like the ships' own cats.
But far from this uncertainty,
From the raucous peril of the highest seas,
Citizens wonder what will be,
And skittish,
Consider their passports.

First At Last
Intro

7/21/2024

    This poem rejoices in the prospect of so many "firsts" being achieved, in the person of Senator Kamala Harris. That is, if she were to win the Presidency, after so abruptly taking President Joe Biden's place, as Democratic nominee in the 2024 race. The poem addresses the President who is standing aside, and making these firsts, if not fully realized, then at least, conceivable.

First At Last

First woman, first Asian, first Black woman, too.
A bevy of firsts, in the absence of you.
Not holding your ground, you have now stepped aside,
Let a whisper campaign put you off of your stride.
How the wildfire spread, when you first appeared weak,
When you struggled to find words and struggled to speak!
We'd forgive it our friend and forgive it our foe.
But for you: no forgiveness. Not old Uncle Joe.

A culture of youth was by you unimpressed,
While the trumpeters off on yon hill writhed in jest.
And the moment your opponent uncertainty harked,
Smelling blood in the water, he lunged like a shark.
But not only the others betrayed you. The we--
Your friends--have all turned on you, triumphantly.
You did what you had to do, under duress.

ANDREA W LEDEW

You caved to the pressure. You cleaned up this mess,

Which the enemy spotted and jumped on, with glee,
Looking always to profit from our misery.
He became both a hero and victim, in one,
Sanctified in his stance, at the point of a gun.
And although you thought age and your frailty no vice,
When compared to Democracy's huge sacrifice,
Should the other guy win, in abundance of care,
In abundance of caution, you vacuumed the air
Right out of that room. They can't make you feel small
For running, if you aren't running, at all.

So, a woman comes forth in the shadow of man,
A lawyer, a fighter, a woman who can
Form sentences, lucid, persuasive and clear.
The woman who's going to beat him, this year.
What will be the issue? That's harder to say.
Perhaps it will be, that a woman, today,
Can defeat any man in the courtroom, the home,
The street or the boardroom. The kitchen has long
Grown too small for the likes of her. Days when she'd bow
And bend, most submissive, are gone. This is now.

So, he'd better be ready for battle. And how!
Defense of our bodies is personal, now.
No gray hairs or faces will carry this crown.
How 'bout, we all try a distinct shade of brown?
It's time we let high heels and bras raise the mast.
Not your toy or possession.
Your leader.
At last.

Laughing Intro

7/25/2024

A poem about 2024 presidential candidate Kamala Harris' signature laugh, and how many may find it easier to laugh, with her running.

Laughing

A bowl, upside down, is a bell.
At home, making cookies, with babes underfoot.
The silence is deafened by smell.
And, drooling to taste it, as well,
The tiny feet gather, and wee chitter-chatter
Erupts, in a giggling swell.

I mourned in the night for my girls:
Their prospects, caved in, by apocalypse in
All the hospitals, markets—the world;
Their freedom, by old men re-furled,
Like a flag, out of favor; their lives, lacking flavor,
In terror of home and the world.

I wept in the night for my men:
Monopoly power leaves nowhere to cower,

No way to be kind to your kin,
If they lack your anatomy. In
Every cause, calling shots, because, like it or not,
Women's rule is the province of men.

Now, watching her on the high wire,
Trusting her and her talents to strike the right balance,
To survive, juggling bowl-pins on fire,
We gasp and we giggle, inspired.
What she's daring to do seems so scary, poor fool,
And we worry, the worst will transpire.

So, we're reaching this point: No Return.
We are equal—or not. We all count—or we don't.
A republic of humans, who've earned
The right to be present and heard.
Every race, every sex at the Resolute Desk.
Yet, in grasping these cookies, we're burned.

Democracy, brought to the brink.
Still, we pull to-and-fro on this rope, Status Quo,
And we tumble, each time a side blinks.
Can't decide: Should we rise? Should we sink?
Others fervently pray, "May it happen--one day."
And they think this, a huge waste of ink.

But their daughters are laughing, I think.

White Intro

8/16/2024

A poem expressing excitement about the prospect of yet another older white man, Tim Walz, running for vice president. And describing how he charms us, with his simplicity and Midwestern niceness.

White

White, like the winters, way Up North.
White, like a wizard or sage.
Who would have guessed that an old white man
Could spell-bind us, still, at his age?

Call him authentic, call him sweet:
A grin, and a grampa's wink.
Real, from his white hair to his teeth,
Explaining, how "real men" think.

Beside her, his eyes, they match her tone--
Though Joy's not what "real men" emit--
So proudly the Beta, in Alpha's glow.
He's upstaged--and loving it!

In him, we can see our dad, our coach,

ANDREA W LEDEW

Our teacher, at lunchroom time,
Our Spouses, who, weekends, duty-bound,
Report in a uniform.

Some would prefer to see, just once,
An all-brown or all-girl slate.
A Pyrrhic poke in the cyclops' eye,
False victory, over Hate.

But now, we intend to *win*, not place.
No points here, for grace or for style.
No weather-days, no forfeits, no draws:
A blood sport. Winner-take-all.

So be content with just a few
Small steps for man, leaps, for mankind.
Idealists, we fight and feud
Over trifles, and undermine

Our one big chance to win those back
Who heed the Piper's call.
At first, his message sounded so sweet.
Perhaps it is starting to sour.

White, like the Piper who would return,
White, like those playing his tune.
Our man's perhaps a new shade of white.
Maybe he is really ecru?

This white man's South will not rise again.
He's glad that it's dead and it's gone.
Everyman, everywoman, his countrymen:
Minding their business, mowing their lawn.

Bitch Intro

8/19/2024

A not-entirely-nice poem, confronting the sexism inherent in both our society and our elections, and assuring us that this candidate, Senator Kamala Harris, can fend for herself. Prompted by a comment from her opponent, *that she was only chosen for her looks.* Salute to a great Elton John song at the end.

Bitch

What woman has not heard the claim
She only got something because of her looks?
She slept her way right up to the top?
She is all flash and no substance?

The whiny, cranky schoolyard chant,
"No Girls Allowed"—adultified.
Absent other excuses, please,
Do blame it on our genitals.

Add to our boobs, a new skin color.
See, how the men all puff and swoon!
An exotic woman in the bloom of youth,
There, just to please the men.

Our highest, best use, is as bunnies,

And the innuendo is not lost,
One of rampant reproduction.
Those without babies are suspect.

A woman is only allowed to exist
In the higher spheres, because men gain.
She adds to their prestige, somehow.
Yummy candy, on their arms.

She is only there because of her looks--
Assuming, she's still got them.
A woman past her prime's a dog.
A female dog. A bitch.

No holds are barred, as we cling to youth,
With hormones, cooked, in the service of men.
For, what an insult, to force a man
To look on a face, less than pretty!

Ancient medieval suspicions say
A woman needs to be controlled,
And, infantile, abide at home,
And make do, with women's work.

For women are not as smart as men,
And acting solely on emotion,
They're only good for birthing babes
And cooking and mopping floors.

We know, when we aim for higher things,
We're acting way above our station.
Hard to forget, our station is
Forever lower than man's.

And as for higher office, well,

What gross presumption, what crime, what folly!
To think such factory seconds
Could survive a world of thugs!

And yet, from Cleopatra to
Elizabeth to Merkel,
Mere women have commanded men,
Through times of peace and war,

As well or better than men, I'd say,
As if merit even matters.
For that is the curse of women:
Being good is beside the point.

When has our competence been gauged
By fact and not opinion?
We rise and fall on lewd suggestion,
Whispered innuendo,

A sliding scale, depending on
Which man now holds the power,
Or microphone, as the case may be.
And they say, *we* are fickle!

"You bet, I'd do her!": meant to be
High praise. But should she *lead* me?
Hell, no! That job requires a man.
How subtle, these attacks.

How can one argue with the claim
One's *sex* is undeserving?
A boy can aspire to anything.
But a woman needs consent?

Aren't we tired of perpetual war,

The fight to own our own bodies,
To have a say, in the world of men,
And be seen, and not dwell in their shadow?

Well, make way, lads! You've been led by men
And have basked in the bliss of their wisdom.
That bliss is about to be broken, boys.
This beautiful bitch is back.

Weird Intro

8/26/24

    A few weeks ago, President Biden stepped aside from the 2024 Presidential race, and anointed VP Kamala Harris as the Democratic Presidential Candidate. This was received with spontaneous applause and more or less general acclaim within the party.

    Ever since, the word "weird" has come to the fore. VP Candidate Tim Walz is credited with first having used the term, as a way to describe Kamala's rival Trump, his running mate, and the general movement he purports to represent.

Weird

In Politics

I guess the word "weird" is slightly less insulting than "the deplorables" of Hilary Clinton's doomed 2016 campaign. "Weird" certainly captures, in a single word, how flabbergasted we Democrats are--see Trevor Noah's comedy special, *Where Was I*, for how much white people *love* to be flabbergasted. We cannot believe Trump's continued appeal, despite the fact that his dirty laundry is hanging out, for all to see.

"Weird" helps us put a name to the way Trump's "Republican" party seems resistant to things, which once were norms. The way they spurn progress in civil rights. The way they lambast DEI--diversity, equity and inclusion policies--so much so, that in Florida, my home state, such policies have now been surgically removed from governmental entities, including universities, government hiring programs, and the Florida Bar's Continuing Education requirements.

"Weird" describes to us Democrats the way our opponents are suspicious of government, questioning and seeking to micro-manage even its most basic functions, like holding elections, voting, and choosing the contents of libraries. It describes the way they name and blame formerly nameless functionaries and bureaucrats, seeking to expose some non-existent nefarious motive or political bias.

A Loaded Term

But "weird" is a loaded term. Harken back to those halcyon days, when bullies were allowed to roam free on every school playground. Most people my age, who, as children, thought themselves ordinary, normal, or possibly even exceptional, recall the moment, when they were first called "weird."

"Weird" is the verbal weapon of a conformist culture. It means *you don't belong.* You are different. You stand out too much, and we don't want to associate with you.

This word used to have the power to strike a great blow. For a young adolescent, seeking to find his or her footing in a complex social world, nothing could be worse than being ostracized by the "in" group. Nothing could be worse than being "out."

Today, on the other hand, "out" is where everyone seems to want to be. Now, with so few aspects of our lives private, and so many of our secrets carried out into the open and displayed, loud and proud, "weird" is almost a badge of honor, almost a defense against attack.

Each of us seeks to distinguish ourselves within our groups, both in real life and online. We show off our special characteristics, our diagnoses, our cultural wounds. We proudly divulge to all the world, the ways in which our many disadvantages have prevented us from achieving our goals. As if that somehow exonerated us, from the shame of not having achieved them.

This strange, slightly sorry-for-oneself culture is flabbergasting to white people of a certain age. This may partly explain why some older citizens are drawn to a more traditional, old-fashioned message. Even if its proponent carries the baggage of his own extremes and outrages.

So, I will not be terribly surprised, if the Trump camp embraces the notion of being "weird." *Weird to Them (the Enemy) means Belonging with Us.*

I do find it odd, however, that Democrats--a party that claims to embrace every race and gender and claims to care about every stratum of society equally--are using an accusation of nonconformity to appeal to the other side. Or perhaps they are only defining the boundaries of their own side and telling others to keep out. Which does not bode well, if this is a close election.

Re: Those Who Are Different

One clip of VP Candidate Tim Walz's speech at the DNC (Democratic National Convention) last week has been all over the news and social media. It features not Tim Walz, but his son. It shows the young man, tear-stained, full of emotion, standing up, clapping, pointing and saying (inaudibly, because of the crowd noise, and yet, we can read his lips) "That's my dad!"

This moment of pride was very moving to witness. But then, almost immediately, in its wake, came a torrent of speculation about the son, and whether he was on the autism spectrum.

I had to turn away at some point from this discussion, because it was absolutely *"None of Your Business!"* as Tim Walz himself might say.

But also, because it was too painful. This was the Public—internet or not--trying to diagnose, trying to label, trying to "understand." Trying to pinpoint the problem, stick a nametag on it. To determine, once and for all, whether the son was "in" or "out."

I suppose, in some circles these days, having an autism diagnosis has a sort of cachet. A lot of people on the internet do claim to be on the spectrum.

Perhaps, people thought they were doing Tim Walz's son a favor, by commenting on and hyper-analyzing whatever sparse factual information was available about this blissfully anonymous, but soon to be prominent, new face in national politics. The son may well be active online, for all I know. He may even seek the position of influencer, as so many do. If so, all this publicity might catapult his chances of such fame into the realm of possibility.

But to me, the whole discussion felt heartless. No child deserves to be placed under such a harsh spotlight, no matter how "well-meaning" and "supportive" it purports to be.

But even more than to the son, my heart went out to his mother. Being of a similar age to her, and also having a son, with some of the characteristics of autism, I could feel what I imagined she might feel, knowing that her son was a subject of discussion.

So much of life as a special needs parent is spent glossing over differences, trying to live as normally as possible, apologizing whenever necessary, and even hiding away a bit, because being in public with differences is, frankly, more difficult than staying home.

Outside of the odd Trump speech and pantomime, the concept of 'weirdness" is not bandied about now, when talking about people with disabilities, as much as it once was. But whether we use the word "weird" or not, it all boils down to semantics. No matter what terms you use, *being different is different. And it hurts when people point that out.*

Lone Wolves

Today, I read a Substack article by Laura Jeffries at *Narrative Nation*, where she talked about the shooter who was responsible for an attack at the Dollar General near Edward Waters College, here in Jacksonville. The shooting took place a year ago today.

She said that the *Jacksonville incident was referenced in a manifesto by a recent knife attacker in Turkey*, who had stabbed several people. This attacker was apparently motivated by the same White Supremacist values as our homegrown shooter.

She talked about the connections between the two, the vast online and text networks that such "lone wolves" tap into, and how they latch onto "heroes" in the movement, like the Oklahoma City Bomber and the shooter in Norway, for inspiration.

Her point seemed to be that the "weirdness" that they cultivate, all alone in their rooms, glued to their devices, *is not the product of solitude at all, but of a hive mind.* She criticized the local sheriff, here in Jacksonville, for giving the impression in his public statements, that, just because the Dollar General shooting had ended with the shooter committing suicide, it was over. And we could all rest safe.

Like the hydra with many heads, each replacing the last as it gets lopped off, these networks live on, and continue to serve as inspiration, for those would-be shooters who hope to achieve similar notoriety with new senseless acts.

Most people, Democrat and Republican, would agree that lone wolves are weird. But the point of the Substack seemed to be that *weirdness was not the point. Belonging was the point.* No matter what other people think of you, if you belong, you are, in your group's eyes, the opposite of weird. You are "in."

How much more "in" can anyone be, than when they join the pantheon of heroes aka martyrs to their movement? To be immortalized in this way, however under-the-radar the group's praise may be to the general public, is to live on and reach out to posterity, in an eternal electronic embrace.

Weirdness in Moderation

Some people just crave belonging. And they're happy to be weird, isolated, and even shunned by the rest of the world, if it means that their craving to belong to their in-group is satisfied.

Today, especially on social media, everyone seems to celebrate their differences, trying to outcompete their friends with their idiosyncrasies. But the notion of weirdness still holds some power. Even the most unique individuals recognize how much weird is too much.

I can only hope that Americans will henceforth use the word "weird" judiciously, and adopt for themselves only the most harmless, moderate measure of weirdness. We need precisely that level of weirdness, which allows us to safely choose the leader of the free world, and, in making that choice, ensures, that each of us can get on with our own weird lives.

One More Intro

9/16/24

It has been a rather quiet month for my writing so far. They say the stock market always goes down in September. So, too, does my word count, apparently. And here I am, issuing my biweekly newsletter several days late.

I cannot say my writing has suffered from lack of material. Plenty has happened in the past two weeks. A Presidential debate. A party. A reading of local poets. Another party/concert.

And now, another attempted assassination.

I never thought I would be using alliteration in quite this context.

One More

Another Shooting

For most of my lifetime, assassinations seemed to occur generations apart. I remember two distinctly, though perhaps not through personal, but rather through cultural memories. The first was JFK, whose "successful" assassination shook my parents' world. It affected them more, perhaps, than the later MLK and Robert Kennedy shootings (among others), only because my parents were less liberal at the time, than the hippie generation, which followed so quickly on their heels.

The second assassination attempt of which I was aware occurred early in my college career, when Reagan was shot. I remember that moment of caught breath and horror well, though I had not yet begun a daily dosage of news, and still cannot say, to this day, that I have ever given current events sufficient attention.

Thankfully for the nation, Reagan recovered. Although I was no Reaganite at the time, I too breathed a sigh of relief. As I have, with each of the recent Trump attempts.

No doubt, Presidents deal daily with death threats and are saved by the heroic Secret Service from countless plots. Plots, which would otherwise end tragically, but which, because of their watchfulness, never end up in the news.

But now, in the space of several weeks, we have had two attempts on a former--not even sitting--president. One in Pennsylvania, one in Florida.

We know little of the perpetrators, other than that both survived. One was a bizarre, bullied teenager, the other a disgruntled fifty-plus former Trumper. Both had weapons that, in my humble opinion, do not belong anywhere outside a war zone. Both took place in states with little in the way of gun-safety protection laws, states which are inclined to lean toward Trump, politically. This devotion to Trump is, in no small part, due to Trump's friendly stance toward gun freedoms.

I have written many times before about shooters, and the tragedies that ensue when they get a wild hair and decide to make their mark.

- On Uvalde, I wrote *Fourth Grade* and *Scores*.

- On Oxford High School, I wrote *Bullies*.

- I wrote a tragic parody of the song *Unforgettable* by Irving Gordon, called *Unpreventable Still*, in response to 2021 shootings in Georgia and Colorado.

- I wrote *The Yoke,* in response to the shootings in El Paso and Dayton in 2019.

- My magnum opus is *River of Grass*, an essay in response to the Parkland Shooting in 2018, at a high school here in Florida.

As the Bible says—or so I am told—we reap what we sow. Apparently, there are many verses with this general message, but I like this one:

> For they sow the wind. And they reap the whirlwind.
> Hosea 8:7

The first assassination attempt missed killing Trump by inches. This most recent one on the golf course missed, in true Trump fashion, by only a few holes.

Near Miss

Like many, I have lived a life of near misses. I was born on the cusp of two astrological signs, on the cusp of Boomers and Gen X. My parents could have divorced but did not. I could have been killed in a car accident, but I survived. I could have chosen to remain in Germany, but I came home to go to law school. I could have died from an untreated pregnancy anomaly, instead of having surgery, or bled out, instead of getting treated appropriately, for a miscarriage.

I could have chosen to have one, instead of four kids, and could have gone back to work. I could have remained a practicing lawyer and raised my child or children with nannies and daycares, instead of staying home and eventually choosing to homeschool. I could have married someone completely different. (I made the right choice there, believe me, not that there was ever any doubt.) I could have lived my life, utterly unaware of autism or intellectual disability.

All of us can look at our lives this way, trace the paths that we have walked, back to those forks in the road. Near misses are nearly always painful. They always come with a sigh of relief when we realize that our choice set us on the right path.

Let us hope that this near miss, this *second* near miss, is the beginning of an epiphany for our country. As we all breathe a sigh of relief, may we finally turn the page on our policies on guns.

Untrue Crime

I have some familiarity with fictionalized crime. I have been watching British cop and detective shows since the nineties. I have wolfed down *Midsomer Murders, Broadchurch, Luther, Zen, Sherlock, River, Shetland, Vera, Grantchester, Endeavor* (and its predecessors, *Inspector Lewis* and *Inspector Morse*, dating back to at least the eighties) *Father Brown, Agatha Raisin,* and several iterations of *Maigret*.

I raced through all the *Poirots*, all the *Miss Marples* and all the Agatha-adjacent content I could find. I have gone so far, as to consume French, Danish, and Scandinavian series, including *Wallander* and *Professor T*, both in the original Swedish and Danish with subtitles, and as BBC remakes.

One could say that I watch too much TV. My family would probably agree. But considering the low surplus-energy-level that comes with having four kids, sometimes, passively watching a well-written show is the closest to reading you can hope to get.

I prefer lighter shows. Those that, in addition to corpses, have comedy and wit. But I have the stomach (so to speak) to watch much sterner stuff.

Still, I am not a horror fan. Too much blood makes even my stomach turn. I watch, for the delight of unraveling the puzzle of the detective mystery. I like the high stakes that a purely fictional murder lends to the story. But I do not enjoy dwelling on the event itself. I prefer shows who dispatch with the fact of the murder in the first five minutes, and then, spend the rest of the show solving it.

Motive

Even with all this familiarity with weird crimes in the fictional universe, I still cannot comprehend what mass shooters can possibly have in mind. Their purpose often seems to be to *provoke chaos*. Perhaps, the kind of chaos that incites a race war, as some of the more disturbing manifestos seem to suggest. Or a state of chaos that wreaks some personal vengeance.

Going down in a Hollywood-esque blaze of glory seems to be a common theme as well.

Even when one tries to untangle motivation, it is perplexing. How could anyone come to the decision that *this was their best option*? Engaging as an active shooter takes depression and despair to the very edge. It best resembles suicide. On the shows, they use the term "death by cop." It remains an elusive mystery to me, why anyone would act in a way so diametrically opposed to their own best interest.

Pinpointing a public figure seems an especially risky game, in terms of outcome. Especially, a public figure that purportedly has such a massive following. Even if Trump's chances of winning the Presidency appear to dwindle with each successive poll--and I confess that between the polls that I see and those which are apparently shown on other networks, results may vary--still, the race is neck and neck.

What purpose could be achieved by ridding the world of this man? Some people annoy me, sure. I might joke that I'd like to wring their neck. *But it would be a joke.* It is hard to understand this very misguided sense of public purpose. Could someone think that they would become a hero, through such an act? That they would somehow be doing us a favor? This is a grim business. Humane people do not toy with other people's lives, no matter how much they dislike them. *Wouldn't it be simpler just to vote?*

But perhaps the purpose, again, is not just to eliminate a candidate, but to unleash the chaos that might follow. In this way, the shooters resemble anarchists and terrorists, rather than ordinary murderers acting on a specific grievance. Terror wants chaos to ensue. It is among the most sinister of crimes, in that it provokes in us, as a society, a generalized sense of distrust, a primal feeling that we must defend ourselves. How timely, then, that in the past week, we should remember 9/11, and all the generalized distrust and chaos that followed.

Many suggest that we are not dealing with rational actors. Mental Health is often blamed as the true culprit. That is, untreated mental health issues.

I have a beef with this blanket statement that mental health is to blame. Looking with suspicion at every person who has a difference in mental health is something we used to do. Something that discouraged afflicted people from seeking treatment, for fear of the stigma. Something that encouraged the general public to look on people with differences, such as those with autism or intellectual disability or depression or schizophrenia, as less than human. We have been there before, during the shameful eugenics chapter in our history, the chapter that so inspired Hitler. We do not want to go there again.

Of course, in order for a thinking, feeling person, a person with valued social connections, to shoot someone, they must first regard their intended victim as something less than human. We have often used this tool--degrading humans to "less than human" --in propaganda, especially in times, when we must motivate people to fight wars against our enemies. But such inhumane categorization should not be our kneejerk response to a shooter's acts of inhumanity.

Categorical

This is the danger of our current politics. We are inclined, when shouting over the vast chasm of our differences, to categorize each other as less than human. Those who become utterly persuaded by this propaganda may enthusiastically take up arms for the cause.

But we are all Americans. And on the other side of the first week of November, we will still all be Americans.

The election itself is the one pure arbiter of value. In any other year (except perhaps 2020 or even in some circles in Florida, 2000) we would shrug our shoulders at the result, and live to fight another day.

Why must we regard this one as so consequential? Why can't our vote be enough? Why do people feel motivated to force the process, to tip the scale, to rage against what they consider a false, rigged outcome, even before that outcome comes to pass?

We have survived elections before. They have not always gone our way, but we have trusted that, on the whole, the American people will make a good decision. I am inclined to believe that they will.

There is no need for civil war, or strife, or self-appointed snipers. The system works remarkably well. Much like the clockwork universe, which at least some of our founders believed had been set in motion by a higher deity. Who then, blessedly, left it alone.

We have the best election system in the world, as our leaders, until now, have always bragged. We have managed to get through every election so far and have arrived safely on the other side. The more important side, where lies governance.

An assassination attempt on a candidate is only the most egregious form of election tampering. But generally, questioning elections and toying with their mechanics is a crippling practice, akin to biting the hand that feeds you. It *is trust that keeps the system healthy, and distrust that condemns it.* The system has never failed the nation before, because, since our humble beginnings, we have trusted it to give us a valid outcome for every election.

This is but one more.

Cool your jets.

No More Intro

11/8/2024

 This poem compares immigrants in our society to bees that pollinate a garden. It argues that their presence makes our country more prosperous and bountiful. It laments the choice to make them categorically unwelcome.

No More

Pearlescent crabs:
Unfolding mums,
In pink and harvest hues.
The asters dripping
Down with bees.
A drink they can't refuse.

The honeybees
From yonder hives,
They've settled in this field,
Forsaken homelands
European,
For this rainbow yield.

How too, so many
Leave their country,

ANDREA W LEDEW

Come, enjoy this place,
And populate
Our fertile fields
With every colored face.

And every tongue
And every faith
Flits under every tree,
With foliage
Of every shape,
With true diversity.

And yet, we vote--
A monolith--
In overwhelming red.
Bring us your wretched
And your poor
No more, is what we said.

News from the Front: JaxbyJax 2024 Intro

11/10/2024

Today is my first day home after *JaxbyJax XI*, a gathering in Jacksonville, Florida of "Writers Writing Jax." JaxbyJax took place Friday evening and Saturday, November 8 and 9, 2024, at our main public library, downtown.

Thanks to Kathleen Shelton Gilmore, poet and Director of JaxbyJax this year. Thanks also, to all the directors who have come before, and to the volunteers who helped to make such a gathering possible.

News from the Front: JaxbyJax 2024

At JaxbyJax XI in Jacksonville, Florida this month, I had the good fortune to be picked as one of the readers. On Saturday morning, I shared my slightly spicy story, *Patience*, with a great audience, who laughed in all the right places. Since this was one of the first readings of the day, I was able to spend the rest of the festival in relative relaxation, enjoying the words that this NE Florida town has, either directly or indirectly, inspired.

By chance, the event took place the same week as the US presidential election. As a result, many people there were still shell-shocked by the somewhat surprising outcome, in which Donald Trump beat Kamala Harris. Some of the readings seemed to morph toward darkness, in reaction to the week's events.

One that I found particularly appealing was a densely described horror piece by *Victoria Nations*. It was about witches, piercing through their own version of a glass ceiling. Another piece by *Jim Draper*, local artist and writer, whose swampland paintings are quite extraordinary, told us about his fearsome adventures during and after Hurricane Helene, up in North Carolina. He delivered a powerful message, which you could apply to both climate change and politics: *You cannot count on the world ever being the same, again.*

The final presentation was by Tia Levings, NY Times Best-Selling Author of *A Well-Trained Wife*. Her reading delivered many excerpts, which were perfectly suited to convey the strength of, and the regressive female roles touted by, some very oppressive religious ideologies. These ideologies were among the forces who stood solidly behind Trump, both in 2016 and today.

Her book portrays her escape from the Christian patriarchy. It involves homeschooling, gender role enforcement, spousal abuse, and isolation, all in a Biblically-based, cultish atmosphere. (My review of her book is on *Goodreads*.)

Part of her early journey takes place here in Jacksonville (gulp!) She warned us, that the forces who shaped her experience have not left.

When I asked during Q & A, what she feared most from a Trump administration, she said *she feared that the artists and writers would be rounded up in camps*. She also said that she thought reading was one of the ways to counteract these forces, and that we all need to make a concerted effort to get out of our own echo chambers.

I took from her words the message, that writers and readers can be soldiers, in the fight against narrow ideologies which seek to oppress independent thought.

She said the experience of speaking on behalf of her book, here in Jax, was surreal for her. She remembered standing at a podium in a library in Jacksonville while in the "cult," and speaking out against computers being introduced into the library, a position she now finds embarrassing. Years later, after escaping, she protested in a Women's March after Trump's first election, just down the street from the library. She found it gratifying to be speaking out here again, against the very ideology and cultish forces who had silenced her, especially since now, she is speaking with the amplified voice of a NYT bestselling author.

Quite the journey.

Of course, there was much at the festival that was not so dark and troubling. Last Saturday, the writers gathered for an evening of readings just by themselves, since so often, reading times conflict with one another.

On Friday evening at the library, Michael Wiley and Jennifer Chase each read, followed by a wonderful open mic.

On Saturday, I never made it to the Poet's Lounge, where readings ran parallel, to those in the room where I read. I did pick up several of their chapbooks, though. I also briefly met with authors and poets while grabbing a snack in the breakroom, or enjoying the bagel breakfast provided for us, or at their tables, while gathering books for my own collection. I am truly amazed at how much creative work is going on in Jax behind the scenes. I hope our authorial connections will last well into the future.

I would be here all day, if I tried to recount every reading I attended, and every experience during the festival that renewed my faith in humankind. But rest assured, everyone should plan to make it to *JaxbyJax XII,* next year. Our midsized town is stretching out its tendrils and becoming a cosmopolitan city, even if it does so kicking and screaming. I can't wait to read my new acquisitions. And I look forward to hearing all the words that will tumble forth from the minds of creatives here, for years to come.

Just Wait and See Intro

12/19/2024

This is a poem about not revealing what's coming, until it's too late.

Just Wait and See

"Just wait and see," the showman said
As he began the show.
"No showman worth his salt reveals
What's coming next, you know.
But all will change, I promise you,
And nothing firm will stand.
You'll leave this tent a different man,
Than when the show began."

"I cannot say," the author said,
When asked to tell the tale.
"You must experience, yourself,
The words, what they reveal.
If I should forecast every point,

The book would have no power.
I want you hanging off a cliff,
At least, for several hours."

"The play's the thing," the actor said,
"That unveils, opening night.
The darkness, like a mother's womb,
Will push forth to the light,
And something never seen before
Will grace that trampled stage.
The birth will be transformative
And herald a New Age."

"Just follow me," the guru said,
"To where your future lies.
The way I lead will fill your need,
So be not troubled by
The details of geography,
Precise in longitude,
But focus, and obey my
Beatific platitudes."

"You'll soon find out." The politician
Shrugged the question off.
"Your vote gave me a mandate,
Gave me power and carte blanche.
You thought that common sense would rule?
Instead, self-interest serves.
What happens next, my friends, will be
No more than you deserve."

A Cold New Year's in Florida Intro

1/3/2025

    This poem relates, how in Florida, even in coldest winter, the rot of summer is never far behind.

A Cold New Year's in Florida

The coral laurel bursts with glee
In a veil-y gauze of Spanish moss
And greets the year in drapery,
From greens, to reds, to finally, off.

And like mere babes, we, too regard
The new year, naked, vulnerable,
Its face, without a line or hardness,
Cute and indecipherable.

This coldness: inconceivable!

ANDREA W LEDEW

It rises to our cheeks a blush.
So seasonably unseasonal,
In a place so often hot and lush.

And in our midst, the new newcomers,
Quick, to adopt our lazy swoon.
The warmth so warmly woos corruption:
Freshest cream is cheese by noon.

But for the moment, we pretend
And brace for a blizzard's cold embrace,
As if this snap would never end
And usher in hotter, wetter days.

So, welcome the year with ice and frost,
Our history, unwritten yet,
Till all shall melt, till all is lost,
Till we know, how rotten it can get.

Half-Mast Intro

1/14/2025

    This poem was written in the wake of President Jimmy Carter's death. After a President's death, flags are flown half-mast for a period of time. Unfortunately, this inconvenienced the incoming President, who demanded, for a few days around his inauguration, that flags be flown full mast. There are references in the poem to the Washington Monument, encircled by half-masted flagpoles; to relatively recent memories of Watergate and its famous whistleblower, Deep Throat; and to the wildfires, currently burning in California. The fire reference includes a cameo by Dick Van Dyke, the famous actor who played a chimney sweep in *Mary Poppins*. In a recent news item, he was carried out of his burning home on a stretcher. The opinion regarding President Carter's incompetence is *not* one that I share.

Half-Mast

Flags at half-mast,
Mourning a president.
Fluttering loud
In the stiff winter breeze.
Grouped in a circle,
A patriots' powwow,
Here in his lap,
Where old George takes his ease.

Chopping a tree,
And not lying about it.
Serving just twice.
Not becoming a king.
All that this monument
Represents to us
Shows us, how far we are

From where we've been.

Even the living
Are wrestling with memories.
Sources, met secretly,
Spilling the beans.
Loyalty tested
Against civic duty.
Congress, in hearings.
A leader, in ruins.

Close calls correct us.
We monitor closely.
We pay close attention,
Avoiding a crash.
What needs to happen
To shake us, to break us,
Out of our stupors
Before we are ash?

Whole cities, burning.
A new Armageddon.
Carrying chimney sweeps,
Stretched out and prone.
Loved peanut farmer--
Incompetent, some say--
Welcome incompetence
Back to your home.

Private School Intro

1/29/2025

    This poem discusses how the new administration is imposing limitations on rights, and compares those limitations to those imposed on children, in a strict private school. It suggests that under the same circumstances, our response is bound to be similar, too.

Private School

Children, sitting in straight rows,
Raise your hands before you "go."
Children, walk in single file.
Change to gym shorts, run a mile.
Tiny children, cling to rope,
(This side, yes, and that side, nope)
Walk the halls on right side, tight.
Never know when Chaos might
Break out. We must to rules adhere.
Rules for speaking. Rules we fear.
Everyone must stay in line.
Eyes on Teacher, all the time.

What I do and what I say
Conform, or there'll be Hell to pay.
Painful spankings. Lousy food.

ANDREA W LEDEW

Teacher does it for our good,
Helping us grow big and strong,
Till we to the elite belong.
No crybabies! No complaints!
We must bear it all like saints.
No objections, talk of rights, or
They'll come for us, in the night.

Do we dare to speak our piece?
Not a word, till we're released.
During recess, plot escape
From this wretched place we hate.
What of those who think it's bliss
And bask in such capriciousness?
The teacher's pets, who stock the shelves?
Screw them. We must save ourselves.

Next time, when the Teacher hovers,
When he's screaming "Duck and cover!"
Run, and bend and break each rule!
Or there's no escaping private school.

Left Unattended Intro

1/30/2025

A poem on the dangers of inattention, in a democracy.

Left Unattended

Left unattended and on its own,
A child will wreck and destroy a home.
Left unattended, a car will rust.
A house will acquire a layer of dust.
Left unattended, allowed to flag,
Our bodies will bloat and droop and sag.
Left unattended, the lawn grows tall,
And the garden's a thicket of weeds and all.

Left unattended, a fervent love
Will go off course at the slightest shove.
Left unattended, our tempers rise,
And the air grows fetid with truth and lies.
Left unattended, our insults, hurts,

Will grow and fester and finally burst.
Left unattended, our lonely souls
Will warp and slip into great black holes.

Left unattended, a ship full of plunder
Will drift, unmoored, and sink right under.
Left unattended, a stock will revert
From its highest value, and plunge to Earth.
Left unattended--no human eyes--
Our planet will sicken and slowly die.
Left unattended, our state will fail,
Without us conducting, go off the rails.

So, while you attend to what's on your screen,
Pay some heed. What I really mean
Is, somewhere, a shoe is about to fall.
If only we'd kept our eyes on the ball.

It Should Be Free Intro

2/8/2025

A poem about the cost of free online written speech. And why we should each invest enough, to allow those we read, who write, to make a living. A response to a common complaint against online paywalls. Addressed to those who believe all content should be free, assuring them, that even when they think it is free, it isn't.

It Should Be Free

The laziness of socialism:
Things should come to me!
If something is of use to you,
You want it to be free.
So greedy are those capitalists,
They charge you by the word,
Demand, you invest in their messages,
Pay up, before they're heard.

But don't they know, some messages
Hold truths so bright and clear,
You can't treat them like sausages,
And charge, till they're too dear
For all but the elite to buy

And read with toast and tea.
Such urgent truths harm in absentia.
Thus, they should be free.

But what of those who scribble,
And commit words to the page?
Who foster these ideas that
Provoke your ire and rage?
No matter. If the Greater Good
Is served by making slaves
And pieceworkers of those whose brains
Are drained upon the page,

So be it. Let them pay for rent
Some other way. And eggs.
You want your content free?
Give your I.D. Your arms and legs
Don't interest us, just yet. But we
Will gladly scrape your feed
To learn your interests, buying habits,
Votes: just things we need.

Soon, words will be pre-thought,
Pre-vetted by our A.I. friends.
This free-range party of the
Blood-ed's coming to an end.
You like your freedom virtual?
Real freedom costs, you fret.
If you want something on the cheap,
A knockoff's all you'll get.

Country, In the Strictest Sense of the Word Intro

2/14/2025

Recently, I wrote a poem called *Private*. It centered on my mother, the way she kept her secrets and poems close to her vest. Many children must grow up in the way I describe, bewildered by things they never talked to their parents about, things that remained secrets, even after death.

But today, I feel the compulsion to write about privacy from a different angle. Not familial, but federal. Not emotional or personal, except in the broadest interpretation of the word. More like a crossing of a line. An intrusion. An invasion of privacy.

Country, In the Strictest Sense of the Word

It occurred to me that in the many years since I first began blogging, there has been a constant controversy in the tech world, about data privacy online. Europe passed a data privacy act. California and several other states did as well. In Florida, we have only had one since July 2023. At the federal level, there seem to be multiple laws at work, a patchwork, keeping our data safe. In an era of Siri and Alexa and AI of all kinds, it's nice to know that at least the Feds are watching out for us.

Seeing Through Red and Blue Lenses

Perhaps I watch too much left-leaning TV news, and perhaps if you don't, you should stop reading now. Nothing good can come from cross-pollinating the political parties. Except, maybe, understanding and a path forward.

Republicans and Democrats think differently about many things. Even regarding the likelihood of continued inflation in the future, as I learned recently. A chart was shared, on the podcast *Thoughtful Money with Adam Taggart* ("Investors Too Overconfident & Giddy" with guest Michael Liebowitz on January 9, 2025.) The chart indicated that before the election, Republicans believed inflation would trend up, while Democrats believed it would trend down. Now, post-election, their positions have reversed. While the weight of the chart was disputed on the show, it seems to point to a general principle of polarity. If one side changes position, the other must react, equally and oppositely.

Not so much as a Democrat, but as an American citizen, I feel quite violated by what has happened in government over the past week or two. It is one thing, to lose an election because the other side has more votes. It is another thing entirely, to watch unelected non-experts, moving at warp speed, tinkering with the mechanisms of government. This is occurring without authority or consent, other than the general consent, or purported "mandate," conferred by the squeakiest of all margins, in the November election. Meanwhile, a glacial judiciary struggles to keep its balance, in an avalanche of outraged appeals.

The most prominent and obvious invasion of privacy is the takeover of the federal payments system. It seems to have caused "paralysis by analysis" in the strictest sense of the words, in that, by analyzing the payments system, and shutting down or shuttering other systems while doing so, ongoing processes that seek to fulfill existing obligations are halted. One aspect of law which I did absorb in law school is the idea that, in general, *law applies prospectively, not retroactively*. These actions violate that basic principle.

Of course, I can't pretend to be an authority. I can't claim to even be caught up on current events. Things are happening so quickly that even the news cycle has to pick and choose which items to cover. It is no surprise that many have just closed their eyes and ears to news, waiting for the dust to settle. This much change, this quickly, outside of a state of war, is a lot to endure.

And we shouldn't have to just endure it.

Why Pay and Benefits Should Be Private

But back to privacy. Why, you may ask, should payments be private?

This question would seem ridiculous to most people of my parents' generation. My blogpost *Asking for Help* describes the proud and private way people of my parents' generation regarded money. Although, come to think of it, the Commander in Chief is not that much younger than my parents.

This attitude can be summed up as follows: Your pay is your own business and no one else's. No one other than your boss should know your pay. You certainly wouldn't tell your friends, or your colleagues, who may have competed with you for the position. You wouldn't tell your children, even if they asked. That stuff is private. It is uncouth to talk about money as if it were just some random and harmless piece of gossip.

I was quite surprised when I learned that within our state government, you can easily look up salaries. This is a great tool when trying to get a job in government. I believe the federal system is much the same. For the sake of transparency, many facts, once shrouded in secrecy, are instead hung out for all to see. And the people making those salaries are hung out to dry.

Citizens who don't make as much as government workers may look at a government salary with suspicious eyes. See my poem *Public Servant* for an account of the country's evolving opinion of civil servants over the years. Such jobs--such agencies--may appear to them to be a waste of space as well as money. They may get angry when such information is unveiled. They regard such a ridiculous salary as so much dirty laundry, evidencing the corruption which, they are convinced, lies at the heart of government.

Rarely do they stop to check the salaries of equally competent individuals, in the private sector.

These angry citizens may think DOGE should have unfettered authority, much like the divine right of kings, in rooting out by any means necessary, waste, fraud and abuse. It may seem abundantly clear to them, that these workers' salaries and ultimately, jobs, fall into these categories.

- *Wasteful*, because they make a higher salary than the citizen in question, who is struggling to pay for eggs.

- *Fraudulent*, because the citizen may only just now be finding out this scandalous information, and therefore, it must have been deliberately hidden from him.

- *Abusive*, because in the citizen's view, nothing is even decided by government on the basis of merit or experience, nor is it done, by accident or by chance. Government, as we all know, boils down to a conspiracy against the little guy.

This has been the message, and it has been fully absorbed. Some of its acolytes are more than happy to throw responsible, hardworking bureaucrats to the curb. They claim that they are cleaning house.

People should not share their paystubs, and government shouldn't be in the business of broadcasting this information. Jealousies are too easy to foment. Today's world teems with people who, rightly or wrongly, view themselves as victims. The current administration's strategy only stokes that resentment. Light everything on fire, they seem to urge. The books. The federal agencies. Democracy. Our reputation in the world.

Throwing Stones in a Post-Privacy World

Fiddling with federal payments is very troubling to me. It is dangerous to broadcast this kind of information, period. But doing so in a climate of resentment has the effect of making people into targets.

It is wrong enough, to vacuum up people's personal information, entrusted to the government for safekeeping, such as their social security numbers and bank account numbers. But it is unforgivable to play with lives and identities, without a shred of accountability, procedure, experience, or understanding of how to protect that information. Do we really want to "Move fast and break things," as was the internal motto of Facebook prior to 2014? Even when we're talking about our government?

Should we just accept that we now live in a post-privacy world? A world where we don't mind living in glass houses, because, after all, why would we mind, if we had nothing to hide?

The internet, and social media in particular, is a kind of glass house. We let others view us and let them vicariously enjoy our individual privileges. We preen. We fawn. We parade before those we seek to impress. But we also open ourselves to laughter and ridicule. And, in too many cases, to reprisal. That is, we make ourselves easy targets for people who like to throw stones.

But hey, what's the harm in publishing paystubs? Let's publish addresses and emails, too, while we're at it.

In Defense of a Right to Privacy

Privacy is key to living calmly and apart from others. You can count on it, that the mailman will not open your mail, that the bank teller will not cash your check for himself, instead of depositing it into your account. You can count on it, that the intimacy of your relationship with your partner will remain between the two of you, and that how you interact with your children will remain unsullied by outside scorn or judgment or interference.

Sure, there are cases when this privilege of privacy is abused. Domestic and child abuse must not be tolerated. But we do not invade every home without just cause, on mere suspicion of wrongdoing. Do we?

Republican lawmakers love to point to original intent, to the experience and beliefs of the hallowed Founding Fathers. During the buildup to the American Revolution, the Founding Fathers had their own concerns with privacy. They felt violated by and objected most vehemently to the quartering of British soldiers in private homes, and the arbitrary seizure of the property within.

The privacy of the home was not the only aspect of privacy the Founding Fathers valued. Every communication they sent was either in person or by letter. Couriers had to be trustworthy. One had to be sure they were loyal to the right cause, since enemies were all around. The unbroken seal on a letter, symbolizing the idea that it was to be opened *only* by the addressee, was sacrosanct.

Is the seal on our emails today sacrosanct? Are the whispered conversations we hold-- in a chat on social media, in a video meeting, or even in our own homes and cars, under the attentive ears of smart speakers--are they really kept "between us?"

We see how easily our private information is twisted and turned against us, in ads that cater to our inadvertently-revealed desires. How else can we be manipulated if all the information we have entrusted to government is let loose upon the world, or fed to ravenous AI? Where are the invisible dossiers kept, that are no doubt being assembled against us all?

Now *I* sound like the paranoid one.

Of course, on the internet, it is not the State, per se, doing the assembling of our information. Not the actual government. It is only a multinational corporation with the net worth of a small country. So really, there is no need to be alarmed.

But look at the simpering crowd of billionaires behind Trump at his inauguration. Now, you may begin to worry in earnest. On whose desk, exactly, will the digital dossiers eventually land? As ever, those whose lives have been openly lived, both on and offline, will have the most to lose.

Lemmings Off a Cliff

In just the past year, Elon Musk's increasing proximity to Trump has caused many to flee from the comfortable, character-limited columns of Twitter, to the relatively new Threads.

Threads is associated with Meta, and therefore, with Instagram and Facebook. This is true to such a degree, that I cannot go on any of these platforms, without being scolded, that I have neglected to check my notifications on the others.

At the inauguration, Meta's Mark Zuckerberg joined the crowd of tech bros around Trump. Close to that time, he announced that fact-checking was a thing of the past. This has caused many to flee Meta products, as well. At the time, TikTok was on shaky ground because of its Chinese information-hoovering connections. So, the Meta exiles, who may also have earlier fled Twitter, departed there, too, at least temporarily. Seeking not greener pastures, but Bluer Skies.

A bit annoyed by so much change, as a woman my age is apt to be, I nonetheless followed the herd and opened an account at each of these new entities (excepting TikTok.) I did not close any of the old accounts, though, reasoning that, at some point in the future, the stampede may come back the other way.

Sadly, such online protests-by-defection do not do much, to harm Meta or Twitter's bottom line. Both can afford to lose a few million users, here and there.

What to Do?

Between the executive orders, the immigration raids, the threatened tariffs, and the agency restructuring by Musk and his pimply minions, all these constant threats are producing the desired effect. *I* certainly feel cowed. Why would anyone speak up, in this environment, only to have their head Whack-a-Mole-d, by the closest tech bro with a mallet?

I don't know about you, but I found myself considering ways to close down communication, entirely. To place my thoughts and comments and reactions, poetic or otherwise, into a great vault, for safekeeping. Something like one of those seed vaults in Norway, meant to be opened only after the Apocalypse.

But no. I will not be silent.

If I choose not to be silent, I choose also, that my elected representative--of whatever party--not be silent. It is very upsetting to watch people in power sitting still, twiddling their thumbs and doing nothing. "Can't they see what I see?" my brain screams at the screen. Why does everyone sit so quietly and obediently in their seats, even as the schoolhouse burns?

I was happy to see the fifty protests in state capitols on February fifth. I couldn't go, but it was nice to see someone doing *something*. I hope everyone who feels this way--that they have been violated, in every sense of the word--will do something.

Something loud. Something obnoxious. Something unignorable.

No Response is not Enough

I listened to a recent episode of Steve Schmidt's *The Warning* podcast, called "The Anti-MAGA Playbook." I was waiting for a Valentine's Day poetry open mic near me to begin. The prompt for the open mic was: poetry that you love, written by someone else.

I flipflopped back and forth, trying to decide whether or not to go. Then, I chose a few poems I like, feeling lukewarm about reading them to others. With time to kill, I was listening to the podcast, which had Charlie Sykes, the renowned journalist, as guest.

Steve Schmidt pulls no punches when it comes to Trump. He was formerly a Republican, that is, until being a Republican became untenable. This lends his opinions credibility in my eyes, as compared to those of partisans who have always leaned liberal. It also gives him insight, into which arguments *land* with conservatives. And which do not.

I am a centrist liberal myself, but I regard with suspicion anyone, who calls for us to throw the baby out with the bathwater. No matter which side they are on.

Anyway, Steve Schmidt and Charlie Sykes diagnosed the situation well. They described the strange way so many of us feel now, both people who didn't vote for Trump, and those who did, but never expected *this*. The podcast kept coming back to the question: What can we do?

No response seems adequate.

But *no response at all* is, most certainly, *inadequate*.

I cannot remember all the suggestions they had, other than advice on what *not* to do. They were pretty harsh in their appraisal of the Biden to Harris transition, and subsequent failure to win an election that seemed like it was handed to them on a platter. One takeaway was this: Reminding

Republican lawmakers of their oath to the Constitution does *not* appear to convince any of them to desist from tinkering with it.

Steve Schmidt suggested we be *loud*. He suggested that we make them *uncomfortable*. He suggested that we point out, and elaborate on, and share with anyone who will listen, including the media, every instance we come across in our own life, and in the lives of those we know, where someone is adversely affected by these policies.

Surely, each of us knows someone who works for a non-profit?

Someone who is in a program, such as a school serving kids with special needs, which relies on federal money to pay for needed services?

Someone who relies on Social Security or Veteran's health care?

Or someone who, through no fault of their own, has not yet attained citizenship status, and is now at risk of deportation, without any attention paid to their civil, or for that matter, human rights?

We must each use the platform we have, to convince those we *can* reach--however small that audience may be--to oppose these bad policies.

Loudly. Obnoxiously. Unignorably.

Country Habits

I did go to the open mic. I felt quite energized after that podcast. The same few poems in my hand seemed to have taken on weight, carrying more gravitas, more meaning, than when I first chose them. Many others at the open mic took the opportunity to share their views as well. The poetry of others, some of it quite old, still remains extraordinarily potent, in speaking to our time.

Turns out, we are not the first to feel such feelings, to think such thoughts.

My first shared poem was *Hope is a Thing with Feathers* by Emily Dickinson. If you read about her life or watch movies such as *A Quiet Passion*, you will learn, that she dealt with illness and loneliness and the care of her aging father, and yet, has written some of the most uplifting poetry. We all need to remember to be hopeful and positive in these times of adversity. Despondency helps no one.

The second one was a Robert Blanco poem from his collection, *Homeland of My Body*. It is called "Mother Country."

Robert Blanco is a contemporary Cuban-born poet who was Poet Laureate of Miami, FL, and who was selected to craft and read a poem at Obama's inauguration. He did the keynote at the Florida Writer's Association convention last fall, and read among others, this poem.

It is a powerful statement about the immigrant experience, as seen through the eyes of his mother, who immigrated as a mature adult. Needless to say, I couldn't get through the last few lines without crying. Few people love our country as fiercely, as those who have immigrated here. Our country would be a poorer, less poetic place without such immigrants.

The point of the poem is, that the country you move to--to escape oppression, to seek a better life, to fulfill dreams unattainable in your former country-- that new country that you find yourself in, by choice, is *your country*, in the strictest sense of the word.

Finally, I read a selection from a long metered but unrhymed poem by Vita Sackville-West, known for having designed the garden at Sissinghurst, in Kent, in the Southern part of England. Many beautiful photos of the gardens there may be seen on my blog, in my Travelogue about Sissinghurst.

Vita is also well-known for being the novelist Virginia Woolf's girlfriend, while both women were married to other men, an arrangement much more scandalous and illegal then, than it is today. Anyway, the poem reminds me of the days we spent at Great Dixter, in East Sussex, in April 2023, in a five-hundred-year-old half-timber building with gardens all around. I have a blog post about that stay, too.

Vita's book in verse, *The Land*, begins with the section "Winter." The rambling poem praises the beauty of Kent, a particularly idyllic and bucolic part of South England in her day, and still, today. It is a love poem to the land itself. *To the country.*

The segment I read begins,

"The country habit has me by the heart..."
Vita Sackville-West

One can interpret this line--somewhat torturously, but nonetheless--as saying that the habits of our country have us all by the heart. By habits, I mean the ways we are used to. The things we love and take for granted and assume will always be there.

Like the Constitution.

It is probably no accident, that the word *constitutional*, in addition to meaning "abiding by or consistent with the Constitution" (my definition) also means *a long walk*. For example, a long walk in the country.

The funny thing about these persistent, patriotic, constitutional habits is our loyalty to them. Our deep-set, imperturbable and abiding loyalty. The thing about these habits is that we cannot—*we will not*--let them go. Not for anything. Not for anybody.

Now, take a deep whiff of the air of your beloved country. The air of your *chosen* country. Of your *country*, in the strictest sense of the word. And get to work defending it.

I look forward to seeing the fruits of your labors.

Fire Ants Intro

2/16/2025

    A poem that talks about how messing with people, and taking away services they depend upon, is as hazardous as poking at fire ants. This was provoked by the many nefarious activities of DOGE, Elon Musk's Department of Government Efficiency. Through various draconian cuts at federal agencies, DOGE is turning everyone's lives upside down, from seniors to vets to business people. As a parent to an adult with disabilities, the cuts to Social Security strike me as particularly worrisome and debilitating, aimed as they are at those least equipped to defend themselves.

    Fortunately, many people are taking to the streets in protest. This poem is written from the point of view of those in power, who wish they wouldn't.

Fire Ants

We silence you not
With our trumpeting, loud,
With the deafening sound
Of our gilt Baroque horn.

We silence you not
With our muffled-up ears.
Hoping no one will hear,
We ignore you, with scorn.

We silence you not
By our closing our ranks,
By our saying, we'd thank you
To stay far away.

We silence you not,

ANDREA W LEDEW

Though you call from a tower
At an unwelcome hour,
And beg us to pray.

We silence you not,
Though we know, you'll make noise
And alert girls and boys
To our actions, uncouth.

We silence you not
By enforcing our laws,
Gently muzzling your jaws,
Though you only speak Truth.

We silence you not,
But monopolize air
Waves, make people aware
Of our stampede of lies.

We silence you not,
But we're stealing the show.
Entertaining, we poke
Sleeping giants, who rise.

We silence you not,
Tiny, pitiful ants.
We have taken the stance,
You are not worth our while.

We silence you not.
Crushing you in the mire,
Till our feet feel the fire
Of the fire-ants' pile.

Butterfly Whispers Intro

2/26/25

A poem that expresses a vain hope that somehow, something will change, and things will be right again. Inspired by the bold and baffling foreign and domestic policy moves this administration has made, away from our usual practices and our allies, and closer to the practices of our nemises.

Butterfly Whispers

I cannot see why
You raise your arm,
Stiff at the elbow,
Reaching for fruit.
Not a gesture
We often encounter.
Born of ideas
We thought were moot.

I cannot see why
You grab for power,
Stopping at nothing.
Obeying no rules.
Caring not,

To be checked or balanced,
Casually
Executing,
Like fools.

I cannot see why
You won't answer questions,
Dismissing the press,
Like a troublesome child.
I cannot see why you're
Speeding and grasping,
Ignoring court orders
And running wild.

I don't see the point
Of a shoestring cadre,
Loyalists, loyally
Licking your boots.
Shoving your way
To the front of photos.
Buttering up enemies.
In cahoots

With those whose crimes
Strike awe and wonder.
Under their jackboot,
Crushing resistance.
Heard round the world,
May the tiniest flutter
Change our trajectory.
Butterfly whispers.

Once we were known
As a country of Order,
Of Freedom,

ANDREA W LEDEW

Of Fairness,
Of Law and Free Will.
Now, that bright vision
Subsides into darkness.
Gone
Is our Great City
On A Hill.

Five Things Intro

3/3/2025

A poem commenting on the letter which the leader of DOGE (Department of Government Efficiency) Elon Musk, sent to federal workers, asking them to list five things they have done in the past week, in order to avoid losing their present job, now.

Five Things

What have you done these seven days
To prove you've earned your keep?
We're tired of paying out your wage.
This state's so dark and deep,
And government's a behemoth,
A monster, and a whale.
We don't believe we need those things
Your paltry job entails.

Long gone, the days our government
Sought out an even keel.
Today we whipsaw, turn about,
And every day, reveal
A new side to our government,
Our foreign policy.
Our enemies turn into friends.

Our friends, to enemies.

What need have we for acronyms?
Our ABC's, we know.
No CIA, no FBI,
Observing friend or foe.
We needn't fear, they'll interfere
In any cyber way.
They've promised they would not,
And we will trust them, all our days.

It's not as if this new alliance
Ever breaks its word.
It's always, clearly, wanting more,
And now, it knows we've heard
Its siren call: Abandon NATO!
Let Ukraine be damned!
Be grateful—We are oh, so grateful,
Eating from your hand.

Prop up the government with those
Whose fealty never sours.
Our twist-a-minute prime-time show's
An amateur-run hour.
And while the pros critique, protest,
We'll sweetly entertain,
Until a new pandemic strikes
Or wildfires re-arrange

Priorities. But by that time,
You will not recognize
Your government. It will have shrunk
To such a tiny size,
That I can hold it in my hand,
And coo, and watch it laugh,

And take that darling baby child,
And drown it in the bath.

Porch Protest Intro

3/7/2025

This is a short story, speculating about one way that people can creatively protest various bad policies impacting their lives. Inspired, by upcoming protests against the countless radical changes being implemented in US government and the damage being done to the global reputation of the US. These protests are scheduled to take place April 5, 2025, across the USA and the world.

Porch Protest

When Penny realized that the country was failing, she turned to food, as she always did in times of crisis.

Barely able to reach his young arms around Penny's convex mom-waist, Charlie's big brown eyes looked up at his mother.

"You have an idea, don't you?" he giggled, knowing the signs.

Penny smiled and hugged her young brown thing, apple of her eye. She tousled his brown waves. He would have been due for a haircut, had his parents leaned more conservative. As it was, Penny preferred her young man, like her garden, to look a little unkempt, a little overgrown.

"You better get ready for school," she said, eying the cat clock on the wall of the tiny kitchen. It had been a squeeze for her and Harry to buy this house, especially with Penny staying home. Interest rates were sky high and reasonable rentals were nowhere to be found. Six months ago, they decided to let their rental go, when their landlord once again raised the rent. They vowed, never again to be tied to that particular railroad track, like that storied silent film character, who can't pay the rent, but must pay the rent.

As hard-core liberals—or just "nice people" as Penny's mother used to say—they wanted to be close to the city center. And why not? All the farmers markets were there, and there was at least one cultural happening, at a walkable or bikeable distance, every single weekend.

They were willing to sacrifice a little lawn, to live there. What they ended up with was a dilapidated thirties Craftsman Bungalow with a wide front porch and just a tiny hem of lawn around it. Hedges and fences separated them from neighbors on three sides, and the porch side was open to the street. A rather busy street. Far busier, than most moms with young children would feel comfortable with.

Penny and Charlie waited to edge out backwards into that busy street from their tiny brick driveway, interspersed with weeds. Weeds did not bother Penny. She found charm in disorder. She took pleasure in disruption. Chaos, even. The wells of the car's backseat were strewn with discarded juice boxes, torn plastic wrappers from gummies and cereal bars, and half-sized water bottles. They lay like a mini graveyard at the base of Charlie's booster seat.

The Mini-Cooper couldn't hold much more than the two of them. The car had been Penny's present to herself, when she had a "real" job. An office job. One, in which she worked half as hard as she did now.

The morning traffic would not let up. A string of curses escaped Penny's lips, which were usually more judicious.

"Don't repeat that!" she warned Charlie's image in the rearview mirror.

"Repeat what?" asked Charlie. He was busy playing with an app on Penny's phone. Penny silently reminded herself, with no real hope of remembering later, that she needed to turn off the setting that allowed you to purchase more turns on the game. Last month, Charlie had nearly broken the bank!

Penny eased out into the tiny gap between cars and fumbled with the gears, as more cars honked behind her. This was the price of compromise: a great but tiny house, in a charming but run-down neighborhood, with a bit more crime than she'd like, on a street with constant traffic.

"Bingo!" Penny exclaimed, as she belatedly slammed on the brakes at the red light.

Charlie smiled. "You know what you're going to do!" he squealed. Games had nothing on his mom. Whatever she had in mind would be way more exciting than any game.

"You bet I do!" said Penny. "Just wait till this weekend!"

Penny got on the phone as soon as she dropped Charlie off. She waved at Teesha Gomez, who owned the daycare "Garden of Verses" and made an "I'll call you" gesture, as she drove off.

It was a stretch, to pay for daycare with a mortgage, high property taxes and just one income. This year, now that four-year-old Charlie was old enough for government-paid preschool, Penny took full advantage. She had to admit, she was a much nicer person when she got a three-hour break from Charlie.

As a young mom, Penny barely had a moment to shower, let alone, think her own thoughts. Daycare gave her a chance to devote her full attention to things that required brainpower. Like doing the bills. Or organizing a protest.

"Carol? I'm so glad I caught you!"

Carol murmured something similar at the other end.

"How's it going?" Penny picked up a sprayer bottle and polished the countertops. With any luck, no six- or eight-legged critters would dart out of the crevices. The problem with hundred-year-old houses was that they were generally built like sieves.

Carol emitted a slow moan. "I can't even look at the news anymore," she said, a low note of regret in her voice. "I used to be so engaged. Especially before the election. Now, I just feel useless."

Penny tsk-tsked. "Oh, no, Carol. Don't think like that. It's not the end of the world."

"But it is," whined Carol.

"Why don't you come over and help me plan something? Charlie's at school, so we can relax."

"Okay, cool. Anything, to escape the laundry!"

"I know! I'll call Mildred, as well."

Mildred was named after her grandmother, who was born more than a century ago. She allowed only her closest friends to call her by her full first name. Most of the time, she was simply "Milly."

Milly did not pick up until Penny was leaving her message.

"Hey Milly," said Penny cheerfully. "How about you come over and help me plan something for the weekend?"

"Will there be food at this planning session?" asked Mildred, doubt in her voice.

"Only your favorite chocolate-caramel brownies," said Penny. She turned on the oven light and peered at the moist brown goo heating up inside.

"What time do you want me?" Mildred responded. Her keys jangled in the background.

"Come now," said Penny. "I gotta get Charlie at twelve."

Penny looked at the time on her smart watch, trying to ignore the accursed, guilt-provoking exercise app. Fred should be home by now, she mused. He worked the late shift at a nearby bar.

"Keep my seat warm!' he texted back. "On my way!"

The four cars, tiny and electric though they were, barely fit in the brick driveway. Fred had a bottle of vodka in one hand and a jug of V8 in the other.

"Got any celery?" he asked. His eyes looked red, and a little puffy, as if he hadn't had any sleep.

Fred was known for his afternoon power naps. Also, for his prowess on the piano. Though he manned the bar at the "Flamingo" he also filled in on the keyboard, if any of the bands were shorthanded. Fred was nothing, if not spontaneous.

"How's tricks?" he asked the group, breezing into Penny's tiny kitchen and grabbing tumblers from the cabinet. "Love this turquoise!" he gushed.

Penny's cheeks brightened with pleasure. Fred had excellent taste. Penny had fought hard for that wall color, against Harry's more suburban preference, bone or ecru. Fred's comment felt like vindication.

"One finger or two?" asked Fred. The girls settled for one, as they would be driving soon, and at the daycare, drunken pickups were generally frowned upon.

"Day drinking!" squealed Mildred. "It's been too long. So, Penny, what are we here for, anyway?"

Penny smiled. She held a notebook and a pen. Old school. Her phone never left her side, and her laptop was always nearby, but today, in this suddenly topsy-turvy world, she felt the need to keep her most subversive thoughts on the downlow.

"I have gathered you here, because, I think you'll agree, we do need to do *something*."

"Hear, hear!" said Fred, raising his glass. "To doing something!"

"But what?" asked Carol. "What can we do? Let's face it. We're nobodies."

Fred, swiveling, gave her shoulder a friendly shove. "Speak for yourself, girl!"

Penny gasped and grabbed her phone. "I forgot to call Teesha!' she said, fumbling to enter the number of the daycare owner.

"Jeez. Racist!" breathed Milly in a singsong. She then continued chewing the corner of a gooey brownie.

"At least I remembered!" said Penny in her own defense.

"Teesha Gomez." The phone lay flat on the coffee table, on speaker.

"Hey Teesha!" they all called out. Everyone in the room had at least one child at "Garden of Verses." They all loved the amazing director and her poorly paid but dedicated crew.

"Hello, ladies!" said Teesha. Fred giggled. "What can I do for you?"

"When do you have your lunch break?" asked Penny. "We're having a planning meeting. We're planning...a protest."

"A protest?" Teesha's deep voice conveyed mild amusement. Her follow-up dripped with sarcasm. "Against what?"

Everyone laughed.

"I can't get away now," Teesha continued. "When's the protest?"

"Saturday, during the Farmer's Market."

"Okay," said Teesha. "I'll be there. Wait, where exactly do I need to be?" Children screamed and birds twittered over the phone. The familiar sounds of recess.

"Right here," chirped Penny excitedly. She relayed specifics, how to get to her home, what to bring, and so on. "Don't forget to bring something for your favorite cause under attack!"

"Hmm!" grunted Teesha. ""That's easy. Health and Human Services. They're freezing and delaying my Head Start Funding. That's half my budget! And what about them kids and their working parents?"

The others nodded and drank, with sober expressions, making pitiful sounds of commiseration.

Penny hung up and scribbled. "Your turn, Mildred. What's your cause?"

"I don't know," said Milly, leaning over and tying her hiking boots absent-mindedly. "Wait! I know! The National Park Service! That trip to Yellowstone last year was mind-bending. And the Grand Canyon! How are they going to run those parks and manage all those people on once-in-a-lifetime trips, if they fire everybody who works there? And with no one manning the fort, are they gonna just close up and drill for oil instead?"

"Boo! Hiss!" said Carol. Pen at the ready, Penny's focus now turned to her.

"What, is it my turn?" said Carol, straightening in her seat. "Well, I suppose I'd have to go with the Department of Ed and—and also Medicaid. The Department, which they want to get rid of altogether, helps fund IDEA, the Individuals with Disabilities Act. Jenny has Downs, as you well know, and at school she has an aide, supports, and inclusion. I can enforce her IEP, or individual education plan in a hearing, if I need to."

Carol sniffed and shaded her eyes for a moment. "What if they take that all away? You think our state—Florida—is gonna make up the difference? I can't even be sure that Medicaid will be there when my husband no longer has insurance or both of us are gone, and Jenny will still need it for her meds and her heart. At this point, I think Medicaid helps reimburse the school for some medical services for special ed kids, too. We'd be up a creek without a paddle, without the government help!"

"Oh man. I'm so sorry, Carol. You must be so worried."

Fred gave Carol a little side hug. "What kind of barbarians are running this show?" he asked the empty air. All eyes turned to him.

Fred, fond of a dramatic pause, headed back to the kitchen to get what remained of the Bloody Mary pitcher. He pulled Tabasco out of the cupboard to give his own drink an extra kick. After doling out seconds, he sat, crossed his legs neatly, one nearly covering the other, and pondered.

"The question isn't *what* program I am worried about. The question is, *which* one am I worried about the most? How do I choose? So many candidates!"

"Like what?" asked Penny.

"Okay—there's that whole hate speech thing on LGBTQ+, like they can't remember that many letters, though they sure as hell can remember a seven-digit phone number. And boy, the "T" for Trans is getting the brunt of it.

"Did I mention that the "Flamingo" has drag show on Tuesdays? Not that all trans people do drag, or vice versa, of course. It's just crazy, how they focus on bathrooms, and think that a few teenage trans athletes are gonna whoop their straight asses, as if they were East German Olympians from the Cold War, jacked up on steroids.

"They just want to turn everything back. Time. Civil Rights—Gay rights, Women's rights, Disability rights--everything. All the things we worked for, for decades, gone, on one person's say-so? Nah-ahnh! Not on my watch, sister!"

"Nicely said, Fred. I expect some very colorful signs on Saturday." Penny patted his knee approvingly.

"You can count on me," said Fred. "Hey Penny. I've been meaning to ask. Is it okay if I bring my friends?"

Penny froze for a minute. What was this thing she had started? Was it getting out of hand? Was she biting off more than she could chew?

She took a deep breath and set down her pen.

"Yes," she said. "Of course you can. The more the merrier."

They clinked glasses at the thought. For the next hour, they chatted among themselves, talked about who they might invite, what would be needed in terms of chairs, facilities. Wondering, each of them, excitedly: What if it ballooned? What if it grew enormous, went viral? Not online, but in a real, physical way—a pestilence of protesters, crawling from here to the farmer's market, chanting, carrying signs.

"We can't worry about that now," said Penny, turning over, in her spiral notebook, the fourth page of her possible guest list. "I'm just putting it out there on social media and inviting all my friends."

"And we'll invite ours," said Carol, decisively. Her demeanor and overall mood seemed to have changed for the better since hearing the plan.

They sat silently together, shivering slightly, even though there was no wind. It was much like the feeling Penny had had in junior high, when she had first dared to skip school. There was something outrageously blasphemous about fighting the institutions of government, the people who made all the rules and held all the cards. So much, so very much, could go wrong.

Mildred's face fell. "But what about food?" she asked Penny desperately.

Penny imagined the masses, the crowds, that must have gathered around Jesus for his Sermon on the Mount, and then clamored afterwards, for loaves and fishes. Even though there were only a few to share, somehow, there was enough for everyone.

"I have a plan for that," said Penny. "Wait for the invite. It will explain. I'm thinking along the lines of some kind of potluck."

The group filtered toward the door as the hour hand clicked relentlessly toward twelve.

"See you Saturday morning," Penny said, as she hugged each of her friends goodbye.

"Wait!" Mildred said as she turned around to stare at Penny. "You never told us! What's *your* favorite cause?"

The others eyed Penny inquisitively.

"Isn't it obvious?" Penny asked, laughing. "What I care about is what we all care about. The First Amendment. Which includes Free Speech and Freedom of the Press. But sometimes people forget. It also includes *'the right of the people, peaceably to assemble, and petition the Government for a redress of grievances.'* In other words..."

"The right to raise Hell!" called out Fred. "I'll drink to that!"

And with that, the cars whipped out in a line, Fred backing up and holding a space for the others to back up and take the road. Meanwhile, the cars honked viciously and vindictively, like irritable little trolls lined up behind him for blocks and blocks.

The day of the Porch Protest had come.

Penny's closest friends arrived first. Each carried a covered dish, with children and spouses carrying signage, waving tiny American flags excitedly, and sniffing the air, as they encountered an infinite collection of diverse and wonderful smells.

With a little help from Harry, her husband and little Charlie, Penny had taken a few old white sheets and torn them into three-foot by six-foot banners, which she hung under the eaves of the porch. On one side, in bright red letters, it said, "Porch Protest." On the other, it said, "Honk for Democracy!"

At seven a.m., the road was still fairly quiet, but occasionally a horn would be heard, causing the children--and by now, there were at least ten—to scream and giggle and wave their little flags, as if their lives depended on it.

Penny's house was on the direct route to the Farmers Market, which was just a mile away. The Market opened at seven thirty. Already, trucks full of produce were passing, and people were looking curiously at the evolving scene on Penny's front porch.

The house had a low, white picket fence along the sidewalk, and only a few feet of lawn behind it. The gate clacked uncontrollably every time a truck whizzed by. When traffic stopped at the red light, at the end of the block, there was more curiosity, more horn-honking. Occasionally, they heard cussing or shouts of "Lib-Tards," to which Carol would react with extreme distress, rushing to cover the ears of her twelve-year-old daughter, much to Jenny's own surprise. "I can take it, Mom," Penny heard her say.

"*You're* not stupid—*they're* stupid," Carol growled, in her best Mama Bear voice. Jenny ignored her and continued to listen to Fred on the piano keys, just on the other side of the porch wall. He was playing jazzy, patriotic tunes like "When the Saints Come Marching In."

More people came as the morning wore on, and they brought more covered dishes. Signs went up all over the tiny patch of front yard, like oversized plant labels stuck deep in the ground, as if to show which invisible aspect of your government was planted, where.

A few youngsters took their signage close to the curb. One teen was nailed in the chest by flying citrus, from someone who apparently did not agree. His shirt, thereafter, had a big splotch of orange in the center of a red circle with a diagonal crossing over it, covering the word "Fascists." When it happened, the teen looked up and shouted after the citrus-pitcher, "Good Aim!" The crowd clapped.

Penny took Harry's hand and toured the tables on the perimeter of the porch, where a hundred dishes waited to be consumed, each styling a fancy place-card proclaiming its name. Almost as if each were an esteemed guest at a State Dinner.

Each dish showed support for government, such as it once was, anyway. It reminded Penny of Brownies, and the yearly celebration of the nations of the world. Each troop chose a nation to highlight, and decorated their booth with interesting facts, maps, trinkets, and most important of all, food.

Today, the tables displayed a panoply of riches, commemorating invaluable services rendered, often at ridiculously low pay, and with no thanks at all, by men and women who just wanted to serve.

The tables were covered with dishes like Liberal Lemonade, Antifascist Antipasto, Protest Pasta, Civil Servant Citrus Salad. There was Immigration Ice Cream, Choice Cheeseboards, LGBTQ Alphabet Rainbow Cookies, NATO Nacaroni and cheese. There were DEI Donuts, Department of Ed Edibles, PEPFAR Pepperoni Pizza, Rule of Law Lasagna and

Medicaid M&Ms. Finally, at great expense, due to the newly announced border tariffs, there were Canadian Pancakes with Maple Syrup, and Mexican Tariff Tacos.

On one end of the porch there was a makeshift bar, serving mixed drinks with names like "Cognitive Dissonance," "The Dictator Disruptor," "The Moscow Fiddler" and "Resistance Rum Toddy." A game of "Darts for Democracy" had broken out. Somehow, a photo of Our Fair Leader had gotten pinned to the dartboard, to the great delight of all who landed a shot.

Close to Noon, when the Farmer's Market was supposed to close down, Penny stood on her porch and counted. There were twenty gathered on the porch and steps, and another twenty in chairs, surrounded by signs, in the wee front yard.

Beyond the white picket fence were a good fifty people, few of whom she had ever met, walking in a wobbly but unending ellipse, down to the stoplight corner and back. The marchers were smiling, laughing, waving and jeering at those who threw curses or yelled at them. The thunder of horns, responding to the sheet-banner, "Honk for Democracy," was deafening.

Red and Blue lights, prefaced by a siren, brought the parade of car traffic over toward the center island. A cop car pulled up on the grassy swale and sidewalk, in front of Penny's house.

A husky officer emerged, creaked to a stand, and let himself through the gate with a bang. The chanting stopped. The marching stopped. The tinkle of piano keys slowed, from bubbly ragtime to a single, out-of-tune note, to shrill silence.

Penny moved between the people on the crowded porch until she found Harry, stuffing himself with a Mexican tariff taco. She grabbed his free hand nervously.

"Now. Which one of you is Penny Farnsworth?" the officer drawled. His red face wore a transparent sheen of sweat even though the weather was mild. He stroked his thick mustache with the web of flesh between his thumb and forefinger, and lifted his sunglasses, the better to see his prey, on the shady porch.

"Uh, that would be me, Officer," said Penny in her most polite, most respectful voice. Nothing to see here, she wanted to shout. But she didn't. She knew there were consequences to direct action. And she would accept them.

Teesha, close to the front door, opened her eyes wide in compassion. She clutched her own brown sons to either side.

The officer put his hands on his hips, his stance wide and intimidating. Instinctively, everyone backed away an inch or two.

Everyone, that is, except Charlie.

He wiggled his way between the officer and Penny. Penny grabbed Charlie's shoulders to steady her as she swayed slightly, under the stress of the moment. True, her son's father's family *had* come from Mexico generations ago, but Charlie was nowhere near as brown as Teesha's kids. Not so brown, that Penny had felt the need to give him "the talk." At least, not yet.

As a white woman, Penny herself had no inordinate fear of policemen. But now, with a brown son, with the current administration so eager, to deport all who were not lily-white, well, no one could feel safe. No one was exempt.

"Are you a policeman?" asked Charlie brightly. His voice, like a ray of sunshine, cut through the cloud that had settled over the party.

The officer looked down and smiled. "Why, yes, I am."

"So, you're the one in charge of making sure that people obey the law, right?" persisted Charlie. Penny wore a thin grin of parental embarrassment.

The officer focused on Charlie. "Why, yes I am," he said again. "I don't do anything to law-abiding citizens like you, young man." His gaze darted around the porch in general condemnation. He didn't seem so sure about the rest of them.

"Well, Mr. Policeman, said Charlie, "If you've come here to make sure people obey the law and to put people in jail, I hate to tell you this, but..."

The officer nodded. "Go on."

"You're in the wrong place."

The policeman pulled his head back with a quizzical look. He seemed a little hurt by Charlie's comment. In a more official, less friendly voice, the officer asked, "What exactly do you mean, son?"

Penny's breath caught in her throat.

Charlie smiled, happy to explain. "Well, you see, officer, this is just a party. We are *celebrating* the law, not breaking it! We even have flags. And you gotta see…just come look at all these delicious American things!"

Charlie then proceeded to take the officer by the hand, on a trip around the world of government agencies and foundational democratic principles. All of them, currently in dire jeopardy of being eaten.

When they finished their tour, Penny was still frozen on the same spot, slowly squeezing all the blood from Harry's hand.

"So, you see," continued Charlie, in a very authoritative, though certainly not authoritarian, voice, "there aren't any lawbreakers here, only law appreciators. Law lovers, you could say."

Penny grabbed Charlie's shoulders again, pinning him against her body. "That's enough now, Charlie."

The officer got down on one knee in front of Charlie and said, "One more thing, young man."

"Yes, sir?" said Charlie.

"If there ain't no lawbreakers here, can you tell me where I might go and look for some? So I can do my job, I mean?"

Charlie didn't skip a beat. "Oh, that's easy," he said. "Try the White House."

Penny gulped. The crowd on the porch froze, watching.

The officer stood up with some difficulty. He looked around with a suspicious eye. To Charlie, he said, "All righty then! Thank you very much, son, Ma'am, all y'all. I'll be sure to try there."

The officer sailed down the steps with the crowd parting before him. He reached the gate, and turned around, to address Penny.

"Oh, and Ma'am. If you could please, just make sure to *tell me* next time you have one of these—parties."

"Oh, of course, Officer. Yes Sir."

"You'd better," the officer intoned, looking around meaningfully at the sea of worried faces. "How else can I bring my famous Cop-killer Cupcakes?" he guffawed.

The crowd cheered, waving and saluting at him, as he left in a sea of incessant honks.

Penny breathed again. Teesha winked at her from across the porch. Harry kissed the top of Penny's head and then turned back to the taco spread, cradling his crushed hand.

Penny pivoted Charlie's shoulders so that he faced her. She knelt in front of him, just as the officer had done. Charlie squirmed, resisting her tight hold, her refusal to let him do what he wanted, to play with the other kids in the yard.

"My darling boy," she said, shaking her head. Ignoring her hosting duties, she held the future of the whole world in front of her, like a jewel, and took her time, admiring it.

"Have I ever told you, Charlie, that you are the best boy in the whole world?"

Charlie wiped his hair out of his eyes with the back of his hand and responded in a bored and patronizing tone. "Yes, Mom. *Hundreds* of times. Can I go now?"

Relaxing, at last, her iron grip, Betsy set him free.

Playing Cards Intro

3/13/2024

    A poem about playing with people's lives and government, as if they were stakes in a card game.

Playing Cards

We're prey to the force of gravity,
Weighed down, pulled by your hand,
Interred in some dark cavity
You've dug, deep in this land;

Cut low, by pairs of pinking shears,
By tech bros' cyber-scythes.
Jack Sprat, who has no taste for fat,
Now cuts lean, with his knives.

As airplanes fall from skies above,
And Main Street's pink with slips,
And signs read, "Now Eggs Cost Ten Bucks,"
We protest, hands on hips.

You play a game of cards with men,

ANDREA W LEDEW

Our lives, mere hearts and clubs,
And though you're holding all the cards,
You deal us only duds.

It's hardly chess, you're playing here.
Some say it's more like craps.
You taunt our nicest neighbors
While our enemies enrapture

You, and twist you round
Their finger, useful idiot,
Releasing criminals,
Adoring traitor-patriots.

And while you sell the motherlode,
So quickly and so cheap,
Our people lose their patrimony,
All the world, its peace.

All hail, dear leader of the free!
Come save us from this fall!
Oh, wait. My bad. It's only you.
A man too weak, too small.

Radio Free Europe Intro

3/16/2025

A poem about treating enemies like friends and friends like enemies, in a world that has depended on our constancy for fifty years. Prompted by the administration's about-face on Ukraine and wooing of Moscow, as well as on the shuttering of *Voice of America* and its arm, *Radio Free Europe*.

These institutions famously helped inform those trapped in Communist countries during the Cold War, with radio broadcasts and leaflet drops, containing news that might cause them to hope, and to believe that things could change. Having lived in Germany while part of it was behind the Iron Curtain, I feel pain at the loss of these entities.

Radio Free Europe

Who can write with their hackles up,
With their body geared, for fight or flight?
How can we, as a force, unite,
With demons, everywhere, at once?

Where is safe, when United States
Can no longer hold the World's respect?
France? Utrecht? As you might suspect,
Many salivate, to take our place.

Lobbing bombs and omitting comms,
We now wave *Free Radio* goodbye.
Falling walls gave us, once, a high.
Now, see, how nigh to Them we've come.

Has the world done a sudden twirl?
For no longer, do we side with Right.
Acronyms, stolen in the night,
And despite this theft, our flags unfurl.

Planning well, our abuser "tells"
Very seldom, in this poker game.
Powerful, bluffing without shame,
He declares, "all in." Hey, what the hell,

Men like him can afford to lose.
They've got trillions in some offshore bank,
Or a store of meme coin, to inflate
And repatriate on the isle they choose.

We, less lucky, instead are stuck
With a broken country, shattered glass.
They pity us, now it's come to pass,
And they scatter leaflets from above.

Lunatic Intro

3/18/2025

A poem about the difference between being an Absolute Monarch by Divine Right and being an American President, with all the pesky, inconvenient processes which democracy demands. Prompted, by an ongoing skirmish between a federal judge and the President, on the subject of deportation *without due process,* in which the President flirted with noncompliance of the court's order. (*An update to this story, yet unresolved, is found later in this collection, in the poem Scream.*)

The poem is told from the point of view of a would-be King.

The King Charles portrait referred to, is of Charles II of England, *not* the current King, Charles III. (Charles I, Charles II's father, was executed by his subjects during the English Civil War, resulting in a short period of Parliamentary rule, before Charles II regained power.)

Habeus Corpus is an action developed in England around the time of Charles II, demanding the *return of the body* of someone, who has been placed under detention without process. Sun-King refers to the French

King Louis XIV, a big believer in the divine right of kings, and the one to whom is often attributed the phrase "L'Etat, c'est moi," (I am the state.)

These historical details were cobbled together from a video, seen once on social media before disappearing into the void, and from various searches online. So, please forgive any errors, committed due to my woeful ignorance of British and French history.

Lunatic

Lunatic! This would-be king
Declares His judge a lunatic.
I deify—I mean, defy—you.
Be impeached, you heretic!

To say, that *anything* I do
Is extra-law--beyond the pale!
What I have ordered *must* be done.
I *am* the law, you lowly snail!

My royal portrait soon shall be,
I think, like Charles, his knees spread wide,
Revealing bloomers: finest silk.
Adorned, to fend off regicide.

For what preceded Charles's pomp?

A civil war. Such peasant strife,
And discord brought us *Habeus Corpus*,
Plaguing dear Charles, all his life.

I'm fond of gold. I'm fond of riches.
Royalty would suit me fine.
Adorned with jewels and shiny britches,
Sun-kings make a country shine.

Perhaps some find such aims outdated.
My regime shall set them straight!
Undeterred by simpering Congress,
There's no boundaries on my State.

So what, if I take men, so craven,
Bound and shaved, to jails abroad?
Your written order came too late
To change their fate, despite your "laws."

You say that I am "in contempt."
Who's more contemptible than me?
From highest highs, I *do* despise.
L'Etat, c'est moi, Land of the Free!

Insecure Intro

3/26/25

    This poem laments how the reputation of our country is slipping away, and along with it, our security as a nation. This poem follows on the heels of a lapse of security by the heads of several agencies, on a group chat on the encrypted app *Signal*. The encryption did not meet the security standards required, to date, of members of the US government in such discussions. In addition, a journalist was accidently added to the group (oops!) despite the fact that they were openly discussing upcoming and ongoing defense matters. In the press, the incident has affectionately become known as "Signalgate."

Insecure

Here, we were born with invisible borders,
Unobstructed by human hands.
Other nations have envied our acreage,
Crammed, as they were, in foreign lands.

There, they had history. Knights, medieval.
Kings with power, unchecked, unhinged.
Change came to them in sober increments,
Peppered by wars, wasting kith and kin.

Across an ocean of naïve fathoms,
We have forgotten the tyrant's heel.
Blissful in apathy, buffered by systems,
Now, all our ignorance is revealed.

Now, we applaud the collapse of structure.

ANDREA W LEDEW

"Burn it all down!" we are heard to say.
Pay no regard to widows and orphans:
Collateral damage we're willing to pay.

As long as we reach the desired outcome,
Never you mind, the process denied.
Never you mind, the breach in our safety,
Assuming we win, on the other side.

Led by buffoons and scorned by allies,
We, their old friends, have lost our allure.
Once, we defended them from their enemies.
Now, it is we who are insecure.

In a Red District (Represent) Intro

3/28/2025

    This poem expresses the frustration of voters, especially in Republican (Red) districts. Constituents are showing up in the thousands at town halls and protests, but their elected representatives are nowhere to be seen. I can see this rhythmic poem becoming a chant at rallies, accompanied by clapping, with the first three lines as the call, and 'Represent" as the response.

In a Red District (Represent)

In this country, bold and true,
There's but one thing you must do,
Though your voters yell at you:
Represent.
Represent.

As a puzzle's incomplete
Without each piece, just so, we need
You to be our voice and speak.
Represent.
Represent.

Greek democracy was pure.
Each one, equally, an ear
And each a voice. You're our voice, here.
Represent.
Represent.

Our Republic don't come cheap.
Make it one that we can keep.
Do your duty to your people.
Represent.
Represent.

Though elected red or blue,
You stand for us *all*. You do.
Not just those who think like you.
Represent.
Represent.

You evade and skirt and flee.
You dislike our company?
Do you fear a primary?
Represent.
Represent.

Quiet, still, as if entombed.
Cardboard cutouts in a room.
Shameful. Virtual, on Zoom.
Represent.
Represent.

Hiding out, you hide your eyes,
We see plainly, wherein lies
Your loyalty. There's no disguising.
Represent.

ANDREA W LEDEW

Represent.

Who elected you? Not he!
Whom you represent is We.
To *us* you owe your loyalty.
Represent.
Represent.

Congress is no rubber stamp.
You are paid to be, and amplify,
Our voice! So do it, dammit!
Represent.
Represent.

When we call, no answer. Give
Us credit. Would you have us live
On hold? Your presence you must give,
Or step down,
Representative.

Liberation Day (April 2, 2025) Intro

4/3/2025

This poem marks the occasion of Liberation Day, April 2, 2025, a new holiday heralded by the Administration to mark the announcement—after the stock market had closed at 4 p.m.—of broad-reaching tariffs. The Dow dropped significantly overnight and in the week that followed, in response. The eventual impact of the tariffs is yet unknown.

Liberation Day (April 2, 2025)

Liberate the masses!
Simple rules are done!
Till now, predictability
Has had a decent run.

Tariffs on our autos.
Tariffs, high and low.
Crush us under mounting costs!
Watch the market ebb and flow!

No more safe retirements,
Relaxing by the sea.
Better, to unsettle,
And control us through uncertainty.

Who has time to stop you
From taking what is ours?
We soon will all need second jobs.
You liberate us from our dollars.

Foreign friends convey
A peeved belligerence.
Why be true, when we betray?
You liberate us from our friends!

Born and bred in Liberty,
We know that none is free, alone.
Treating friends like enemies,
You'll liberate us from our home.

Doors and Windows Intro

4/6/2025

    This poem warns us how a country, like a house or castle, can fall far and quickly, when people fail to unite and defend it. Inspired, by the whirlwind pace of change in our country, change, that seems to be occurring in the absence of a proportionately swift and powerful resistance.

Doors and Windows

Living in this edifice
I've lived in all my life,
I never thought the walls would fail,
Confusing, bringing strife
And enmity, among a people
Meant to act as one,
Against all forces, here, abroad,
Who'd wreck our happy home.

I hear them at the windows now,
They're jimmying the locks.
I hear them at the back door,
Pushing, pulling. And they walk
Upon the roof. I fear these sounds

That threaten all I am.
And from the front door, there's the
Rhythmic throb of battering rams.

With many great lands 'round the world
Now scorning Freedom's gaze,
Why should we wonder, that such hordes
Come here to spread malaise?
Our younger kin, they look to us,
To keep them safe and sound.
Instead, we batten down our doors,
Invaders all around.

What hurts me more than watching
As they breech our fort with lies,
Are all our allies, looking on,
With pity in their eyes.
The wickedness is everywhere.
What hope now, to be free?
They're trying all the doors and windows
Of Democracy.

Scream Intro

4/16/2025

 This poem charts the machinations of some ongoing cases against the US government, having to do with the mass transport of certain South Americans. The individuals were residing in the US but were somehow deemed undesirable (something to do with tattoos and gangs.) And so, they were rounded up and sent to an El Salvador Prison, and the US is paying for their upkeep *by contract* with the government of El Salvador.

 Now that they are abroad, the US government claims *they have no way of bringing them back*. The Supreme Court has also put its two cents in, saying due process *was* denied, but also, that the judge can't force the government to do anything in the foreign sphere, since foreign relations are in the domain of the President, not the judiciary.

 Heaven forbid, that anyone should violate the separation of powers! The sarcasm is warranted, since this administration has been doing nothing but testing the boundaries of its executive power, from Day One.

Per the Supreme Court, the judge can only ask the government to *facilitate* a resolution. Meanwhile, ordinary American citizens smell a rat. I have conflated the details of a few cases into one. Not that anyone really knows the details, at this point. My heart goes out to the families of these abducted men and, of course, to the men themselves.

Scream

Sitting in the car, I see
The flashing lights in blue.
Fearing nothing, I just wonder,
Now what did I do?
My hand strays to the hand
Of my dear wife who sits beside.
Autistic son sits in the back,
So gleeful for the ride
And chance to see the neighborhood.

I roll my window down,
Present my license, registration,
Feeling like a clown.
He asks me now, to step outside.
I know I must comply—
Too many men, with skin this shade

Or darker daily die

This way. But then, the cuffs are on.
I'm patted, whisked away,
With barely time to mouth goodbye
To those I love, who pray
And call to me. My son, he screams.
My wife sheds knowing tears.
A citizen, she can't protect me,
Married, all these years.

Protected once by yonder flag
That sheltered me and you,
It won't prevent my kidnap now,
By thugs, parading blue.

I have arrived. The plane touched down.
Two hundred are onboard.
Each sporting the same skin of brown,
Their faces looking toward
The door. And then, it opens.
The equator's blistering heat
Comes rushing in to strangle us.
We ask, where could we be?

El Salvador, they tell us, marching
Chain-gang, heads down low,
Bent over, kept there, thrown off balance,
Hundreds in a row.
They shave us. Men, who look like us.

Contractors for the man
Now sitting in the White House,
With a Sharpie in his hand.

We crowd the bunkbeds, stories high,
All men, some with tattoos,
Some, menacing. And I remember
Fleeing in my shoes,
To get away from gangs
Who wanted me to pay my dues.
Now, like the members of those gangs,
I too, now stand accused.

Not that I stand a chance of trial.
There is no trial, here.
We've all been sentenced to a gulag,
None to rescue, near.
We have no chance to speak our piece,
No right to plead the law.
We're chattel in a cash transaction.
Meaty. Sweaty. Raw.

Back home, the judge, he bangs his gavel,
Asks to know my fate.
He asks, when did the planes take off?
Too early or too late?
The government, it shrugs, for there
Are secrets it must keep.
The judge, he has no right to ask
For facts, so dark and deep,

And dripping with diplomacy,
The president's own lair.
The highest court agrees, you see.
He's got no business there.

The judge can only beg and plead
That they facilitate
A quick release of someone whom,
By tweet, they clearly hate,
They hem and haw, admit mistake,
But swear, their hands are tied—
While mine are raw from metal cuffs,
Here. Laboring. Inside.

The patient judge, he asks again.
Again, they act demure.
He then demands, they be deposed.
They say they are not sure
If they can find the time.
The judge insists they will convey
All news, and drag their clients,
Screaming, to him, on the day.

I scream into my pillow.
Others scream out on the street.
My son, he screams for dear life.
My wife cries in her sleep.
She tells reporters of her prayers
For my safe release.
I did not flee from here

To sleep among my enemies.

Yet all of them were harmed by this,
The guilty *and* the good.
And all of us are starved for justice,
Used to getting food:
Nutritious and delicious portions,
Generously served,
When once, our country loved such strangers,
Lonely in the world.

No more. Now, we are outcasts,
Each, a step away from jail
And deportation. Subject,
To a contract's least detail.
Go ask your leaders: Is it *you*,
They next intend to fail?

Don't ask them for Due Process.
As you know, that ship has sailed.

Pining Intro

4/18/25

 This poem is a call to action, for all those who love their country. It urges us to preserve in it, what we know to be its best qualities, and to defend ourselves, against its worst. It harkens back to the eighties, when I spent time in Germany, while it was divided into West and East. Then, I had to defend Reagan's America, which was not quite as popular there, as here.
 This poem tries to chart the general course of our country since then, and logs some of the very real and valid reasons, that people have acted as they have, and have made the choices they have made.
 But there is no reason to assume, that the American people will allow *any leader* to change the essence of what we know to be our America.
 I hope this poem, and this collection, in its totality, will encourage and inspire people *not to take this, lying down.*

Pining

I've seen my land from foreign shores.
I've lived beneath a foreign flag.
Learned to defend, what I abhor,
And own, those gems for which I'm glad.

The land I daily yearned and pined for—
Sehnen is the German word—
Has morphed and stretched so many times
Since I set off to see the world.

A world of peace. A peace through tension.
Rivals held the tightrope taut,
And nuclear annihilation,
Proxy wars, our Freedom bought.

We thought we were exceptional.

My travels taught, this was not so.
All over, people of goodwill
Led decent lives, helped friends, fought foes.

Yet I could feel their eyes upon me.
All looked to America.
If anyone could fix this, we could.
Fall, the walls of Jericho!

And so, they did. The walls all fell.
We thought our rival gone, as well.
Our world, it prospered in upheaval.
Theirs left but a brittle shell.

It's one thing, to be great in combat,
Honing muscle, through the fight.
Another, to rest on one's laurels,
Dominating all. We might

Have known, that then, out of the trenches,
One would soon take up the slack.
A terrorist—no known location--
Pinned a target to our back.

Secret planning. Plane gyrations.
Towers, flaming. Cinders fall.
Terrorism breached our nation.
Terror gripped us, one and all.

As we limped from war to war,
Depleting coffers, full to brim,
We stoked our hate for all things foreign.
Then, recession nestled in,

And stole our nest eggs. Lost, off-balance,

Fearing certain poverty,
We begged that heroes in our midst
Restore our wealth and dignity.

And yes, we found them. Many heroes,
Trading off the red and blue
Each term, and working miracles,
Until their remits ended, too.

Our hero, now? An entertainer,
Red-capped huckster, hugging flags.
One whose boundaries won't contain him,
Who disdains this great, great land.

Here we lie, a shattered Union.
Compromise, a distant thought.
Government now stokes rebellion,
Breaks its promise, left and right.

Allies look with scorn and wonder.
Enemies prepare their arms.
Are we weak? *Our* mighty country?
Most, complacent. Some, alarmed.

Rise together, *all* my brethren!
Claim the legacy that's yours!
Defend your land, so your children can
Still pine for it, from foreign shores.

The Author: Andrea W LeDew

Andrea W. LeDew lives and writes in Jacksonville, Florida. She is a two-time graduate of the University of Florida, in English and in Law. She spent nearly a year abroad, before the Wall fell, studying at the University of Wuerzburg, in Wuerzburg, West Germany. She has worked as a lawyer, a homemaker, and as a mother of four. For ten years, she was the homeschool parent-teacher of her two younger sons, one of whom has autism and intellectual disabilities. She is currently his caregiver.

Writing credits:
- *JaxbyJax Literary Festival* in Jacksonville, Florida, 2023 and 2024. Short stories presented: "*Becoming the Story*" and "*Patience.*"

- One of four panelists on *Self-Publishing* at *PoetFest* in St. Augustine, Florida, 2023.

- Poems included in four collections:

    ◦ Moss Gossamer: Poetry of NE FL (Happy Tapir Press 2023) "*August.*"

    ◦ Regency Reflections: Inspired by Jane Austen's Work (Wingless Dreamer 2023) "*Us Maids.*"

    ◦ Border Beats Writing Across Boundaries: An Anthology (Border Beat Books 2023) "*Choice.*"

    ◦ Secrets (Florida Writers Association 2023) "*Narrow.*" Fourth Place in collection.

Work In Progress:

As of May 2025, Andrea is hard at work on a novel, centered on a riverfront group home for the intellectually disabled. The Northeast Florida home was supposed to be funded in perpetuity in the landowner's will, but one day, the aged landowner changes his mind and decides to sell. The protagonist, a fiery young woman with intellectual disabilities and no family, is determined to save her beloved home, no matter what it takes. Other characters have different plans.

The path from here to there involves an antique stained-glass window, sea turtles, a devious preacher, lavish gardens, homelessness and dusty old privilege. Some themes include grief and loss, human dignity, and found family. To receive updates, subscribe to Andrea's newsletter at *For Random Learning Comes.*

Contact:

Andrea can be reached through her established website, *For Random Learning Comes,* where most of the material in this collection first appeared. She regularly posts a newsletter and monitors messages sent through her contact page. She also participates in a variety of writerly events. Online, she is active on many social media platforms under the moniker Andrea LeDew.

When not writing, Andrea enjoys the temptations to be found in gardens, old homes, travel, milk chocolate, British murder mysteries, and books. She continues to pay too much attention to the news.

What You Will Find Inside

The collection *Polemics: Political Poems & Prose* takes the reader on a disturbing, wide-eyed ride through the years 2016-2025 in the United States. It highlights the political nightmares and triumphs, both familiar and forgotten, experienced by Americans during this time.

To endure the tempest of the current era, *Polemics* clings faithfully to old-school liberal themes. These are delivered as rhyme, essay and fiction. Its affectionately nostalgic patriotism will resonate with anyone, who has been paying attention long enough to notice, that things have changed. And not for the better.

As Americans try to navigate an America they have never seen before—an America they barely recognize—*Polemics* will serve as an anthem, an incantation, and a call to action. This collection aims to guide their forlorn liberal souls through dark times, toward something better.

www.ingramcontent.com/pod-product-compliance
Lightning Source LLC
Chambersburg PA
CBHW022000160426
43197CB00007B/205